Dave,

Wishing you and

your team continued success

in your quest to achieve

service excellence!

All the best

LEADING IT TRANSFORMATION

The Roadmap for Success

OUELLETTE
& ASSOCIATES

KENDALLHUNT
PROFESSIONAL

Library of Congress Control Number 2008935402

ISBN 978-0-7575-5833-7

Printed in the United States of America
10 9 8 7 6 5 4 3 2 1

Contents

Acknowledgments

A book project is a major undertaking that requires the efforts of many great people to bring it to fruition. While this book has taken the better part of two years to complete, its roots date back to 1984 when we began partnering with our clients in support of their transformation efforts.

We want to thank our world-class clients who include us in their transformation initiatives. We consider ourselves extremely fortunate to work with some of the most savvy IT leaders in our industry; some have sponsored our work at two, three and even four companies. Without them our work would not be possible and this book could never have been written.

While there are too many clients to list by name, several were kind enough to review the manuscript and provide encouragement and detailed feedback that helped us greatly improve the end product. These respected IT leaders include Roger Agee – JELD-WEN, Inc., Ben Berry – Oregon Department of Transportation, Scott Culbertson – UGI Utilities, Inc., Rick Giese – Great Lakes Educational Loan Services, Inc., Cam Henderson – Portland General Electric, Laurie Koetting – Washington University, Chris Loizides – The MITRE Corporation, Deane Morrison – Capital Region Healthcare, Eric Nilson – JPL, Guy Russo – CommunityAmerica Credit Union, Sharon L. Waid – Boston Financial Data Services, Lorena Weaver (ING retired) – Independent Consultant, and Meg Williams – Nationwide Services Company.

We also want to thank our families who support the work we do with clients. Without their support on the home front while we are traveling, we could not do the work that we love so much.

Tackling a book project with multiple authors is a blessing and a curse. It's a blessing because you can leverage the knowledge and experiences of many subject matter experts. It's a curse when you try to weave different personalities and voices together to ensure consistency for the reader. Given this challenge, we want to thank Mary Brandel because without her writing talents, this book would not have become a reality. Her ability to capture our real world experiences and personalities is a gift. Her ability to find a common voice for our readers was incredibly important.

And many thanks are extended to our publisher Kendall/Hunt and their dedicated team of professionals. Fortunately they share our passion for quality and have been very gracious and patient while we labored over every detail until we got it right.

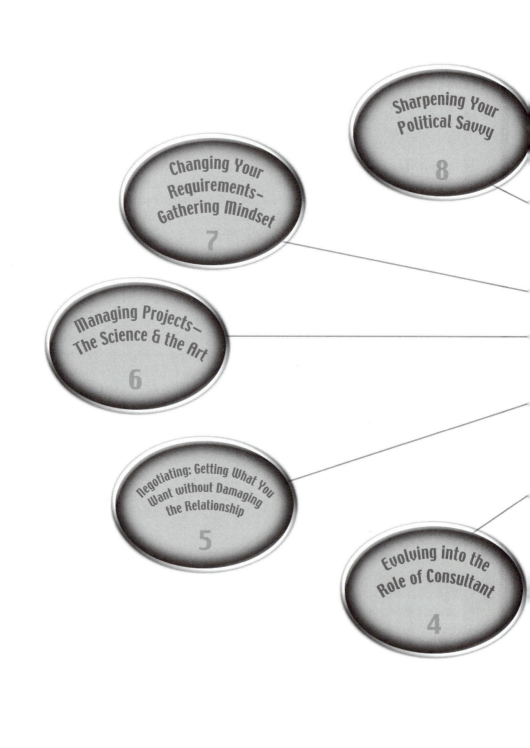

Sharpening Your
Political Savvy

8

Changing Your
Requirements-
Gathering Mindset

7

Managing Projects-
The Science & the Art

6

Negotiating: Getting What You
Want without Damaging
the Relationship

5

Evolving into the
Role of Consultant

4

Marketing
IT's Value

9

Driving Change
with Intent

10

Creating Your 21st Century Workforce and Culture

1

Transforming Your
IT Team

2

Building a Client-
Focused IT Cuture

3

There has never been a better time to be an IT professional. That's right! While prognosticators have loudly predicted the demise of IT, I firmly believe there has never been a more exciting or auspicious time to be in this profession.

That may sound strange to some of you IT veterans out there. You may remember the good ol' days of Electronic Data Processing when IT professionals were safe behind the glass walls, free to focus on technology, without interference from those pesky "end users." Or perhaps you remember being the hero in the late '90s, riding in on a white horse to save the world from the Y2K coding debacle. Then there were the wild, early days of the Internet, when being a techie was suddenly cool.

For those who long for any of those days, I can appreciate your disdain for my optimism. You've weathered the lean years following the dot-com crash, the outsourcing that leveled many of your staffs, the questioning of IT's value and the ROI scrutiny that continues today.

But still, I don't think I'm being naïve. Though the last few years have been riddled with doubt, disappointment and discomfort, they also produced an awareness in most of the business world that technology can be a game-changer. From a business leader's perspective, globalization and other market forces have turned technology into a key differentiator as companies expand into international markets. Cutthroat competition is forcing continuous innovation, and government regulations are driving constant introspection – all fueled by technology. Meanwhile, particularly with the rise of consumer technology, business employees have no patience with "the computer guys" who say, "We can't do that."

At one and the same time, the people in charge of technology are expected to be technologically advanced, business-minded, customer-focused and financially astute. Technology leaders are expected to reduce costs, increase productivity, drive innovation and help the business identify and pursue new business opportunities. In the face of unforgiving competition, rampant globalization and demanding customers, business leaders now know that it's absolutely essential to have a strong, active partner keeping a firm hand on the decisions and strategies surrounding information technology.

Of course, there have never been more options to consider when it comes to doing just that. IT faces competition from internal shadow groups, vendors and consultants, outsourcers and offshorers, all promising to do it faster, cheaper, better. But still, I firmly believe that IT organizations can be well positioned to compete as their companies' value added provider of choice – IF AND ONLY IF they're ready to take a hard look at themselves and make some changes, both in terms of how they approach their work and the personal skill set they consider essential to tackling the demands of an ever-changing business environment. The bottom line is, the IT professional of the past won't cut it in today's corporate world.

"CORE" SKILLS FOR SUCCESS

To remain viable, IT leaders need to proactively transform their organizations and cultures. In order to accomplish this, they need to develop an IT workforce that has the new mindset, skill set and tool set necessary for success, such as communicating, relationship-building, collaborating, managing change, marketing, negotiating and the like. These are the skills that are necessary for effectively filling the growing percentage of IT jobs that are business-facing. You've heard this before, but today, it's no longer just a suggestion; what have historically been termed "soft" skills are the very ones that will drive IT to the level it needs to reach in order to be viable in the future. In fact, savvy IT leaders no longer use the term "soft skills" when referring to these key capabilities. They call them "core skills" because they're the very ones needed to achieve "hard" results.

If you step back for a minute, the need to evolve shouldn't be surprising. The IT profession is really still in its infancy. It's only a few decades old – a new kid on the block, compared to its peers in other business areas that have had centuries to "grow up." I can imagine a time in the future when we'll look back at the second half of the 20th century as the time when IT was just cutting its teeth.

In some ways, IT professionals are now living through the tough teenage years of their profession. They're wrestling with internal turmoil they don't often understand while defiantly ignoring the advice and experience provided by their external environment. Like teenagers, they want so badly to be independent and earn the respect of their peers and elders. However, their erratic, mercurial behavior and unpredictability continue to demonstrate their immaturity.

The exciting news for IT professionals is that they're poised to enter adult-hood. And this new era will have less to do with a command-and-control or bits-and-bytes mindset and more to do with being collaborative and versatile business partners.

POSITIONING IT AS PROVIDER OF CHOICE

That's why we at Ouellette & Associates Consulting, Inc. (O&A) chose now to write this book. We have a lot to offer IT leaders who want to prepare their staffs and organizations for the next phase of IT's evolution and a successful future. Since 1984, our tagline at O&A has been, "*Developing the Human Side of Technology*," and never has this mantra been more important to IT than it is today.

We've been fortunate to work with nearly 3,000 IT organizations representing all industries, led by progressive IT leaders who are dedicated to transforming their organizations, whether their staffs numbered 20 or 7,000. This book is based on these industry pioneers and their passion for and commitment to moving their organizations from reactive, technology-centric, order-taker cultures to ones that are consultative and business savvy – in short, organizations that position internal IT as the business's technology provider of choice.

While other managers immediately cut their professional/organizational development budget at the first sign of economic distress, these savvy leaders invested in their people during both good and bad economic times. By leveraging O&A's IT-specific professional development services, they initiated and sponsored their own personal transformations and then proceeded to help their departments reach their full potential.

A UNIQUE APPROACH

Others have written about the changing field of IT, but O&A's approach is unique. For one, it's written by a team of O&A consultants, subject matter experts and workshop leaders, who for the first time have committed their insights and experience to paper. Together, these seasoned professionals represent more than 200 years of experience in the real-world IT trenches and as consultants and trainers, helping tens of thousands of IT professionals transform how they do business, both individually and organizationally.

Because they've walked the walk as IT practitioners, leaders and consultants, they write with a voice of authority that comes from experience.

On a personal level, I have contributed to several books that have been very well received by our industry. I am extremely excited about *Leading IT Transformation: The Roadmap for Success*, based on the reviews and feedback provided by several respected industry leaders, and am confident about the value it's going to bring to the IT industry and profession.

You won't hear us promoting the latest management fad, promising silver-bullet solutions to the challenges you face as an IT leader. In fact, we strived to write a book that was practical and immediately applicable. How many times have you read a business book, agreed with most everything it said and then discovered you didn't have much if anything tangible to apply? This book, like the proven workshops and services it's based on, is designed for you to begin applying what you've learned immediately. Rather than writing from a 30,000-foot level, we wanted to combine big-picture context with specific advice you can use in your next planning session, staff meeting or client interaction.

At the end of each chapter, you'll find a "top 10" list summarizing the chapter and providing you with immediate, actionable take-aways. We will also prompt you to note a few specific actions you plan to take based on what you just read.

This format aligns with O&A's overall philosophy of helping our clients "learn how to fish." At O&A, we've never been big fans of the traditional consulting model that causes clients to become dependent. This may be good for revenue generation, but it's an approach that's never sat well with us. Our focus has always been on helping our clients become self-sufficient. This book will seek to do the same.

This book is also not going to tell you everything there is to know about IT transformation. It would take several books and more time than you have to cover everything there is to know about this topic. Instead our goal is to help you be effective, to jumpstart your transformational journey, and to build and sustain momentum. If you've already begun this journey, then this book will add to your toolkit and help you continue your momentum. If you're one of those rare IT leaders who've successfully transformed your IT organization, you already recognize that success is a journey and not a destination. I hope you'll meld our experiences and best practices with your own to take your organization to the next level.

We've based the book on proven approaches that generate results. O&A's clients have applied and sustained the teachings in this book, and by doing so, they've positioned their organizations for the future. They've chosen to focus on developing the "human side" of IT rather than "fixing" IT by applying the latest technology, methodology, framework or management guru fad. They've discovered that success is based not on a big-bang theory but by executing many little things every day. These small wins add up and build momentum from the top-down and from the bottom-up.

That's why we believe that by reading this book and acting on its advice, you too can build strong relationships with your business partners and earn a seat at the table of strategic decision making. You too will be perceived as an effective communicator, tactful negotiator and influential opinion leader across your organization. And your IT organization will also be positioned as IT provider of first choice.

A CONSISTENT TERMINOLOGY

Part of the value we bring to our clients when helping them with their transformation efforts is the introduction of a consistent vocabulary. In this book, we will frequently use words and phrases that might mean different things to different people. Therefore, I want to define a few of these here for you:

- **IT.** We will commonly refer to *IT* as the organization responsible for managing and delivering technology and related services.

- **Client vs. Customer.** We will refer to *clients* or *business partners* as those who are the beneficiaries of IT's products and services. When we use the term *customer*, it will refer to the "Big C" customers to whom our corporations provide products and services.

- **WIIFM ("wiff-em").** *WIIFM* stands for "What's In It for Me," an expression we want every IT professional to think about when considering a client's point of view. In other words, find out what matters to the client before expecting him or her to be motivated to act.

- **The Four Cs.** Each chapter is focused on helping you increase your staff's Competence, Confidence, Commitment and Consistency in each area addressed.

Throughout the book, we'll also reinforce some key concepts. For instance, you'll read a lot about the importance of teamwork and collaboration – not just with clients, but also with peers in IT. It's time for IT professionals to rid themselves of all notions of "us vs. them" because to meet the needs of the business, everyone needs to row in the same direction.

Interpersonal skills also come up a lot. In fact, one of our consultants refers to his project management workshops as a "three-day charm school!" Interpersonal skills, or "core" skills as previously described, lead to strong relationships, which lead to trust, and with trust, we can overcome even our most difficult situations.

IT professionals tend not to like the "touchy-feely" stuff, but you'll also read a lot about empathy, an area of weakness in the IT profession. You'll find that empathy is less touchy-feely than you think and is actually a key tool for working through conflict, building relationships and achieving your full potential. It's a matter of listening to the other person's perspectives and letting that person know you've heard and understand them. You don't even need to agree!

WHO WILL BENEFIT MOST

A wide range of people will benefit from reading this book, including IT leaders holding titles from CIO, to business unit or regional information officer, to VP, to director or manager of IT. Whether you are the CIO of a 7,000-person IT staff that spans the globe or a manager overseeing a local IT team, I am confident that you will benefit from reading this book. We are excited to share the experience, best practices and proven techniques that other IT leaders are using to reorient, re-skill and retool their IT workforce and build a new culture.

It's not only leaders who will benefit from this book. Whether you work in applications or the technology infrastructure side of the IT business – and whether you aspire to management or wish to be the most effective individual contributor you can be – this book will introduce anyone on the IT staff to the philosophies and skill sets that will help you meet the challenges of your profession. If you follow the latest research and read industry trade publications, you know that an increasing percentage of IT jobs and roles in the future are going to be client- and business-facing, and we will help you prepare for these new opportunities.

LEVERAGING THIS BOOK

We believe that each of the chapters in this book is important for success. That being said, we appreciate that every IT organization is in a different stage of their transformation evolution and that some chapters will be more immediately applicable than others. We also appreciate that it isn't feasible to effectively tackle all of these areas at once.

Therefore, we recommend that once you've read the book, you identify the two or three chapters that address the areas most pressing in your organization today. Make these a priority in your organization and strategy planning. Demonstrate your commitment and sponsorship by taking every opportunity to "walk the talk" and communicating these priorities to your people.

We also advise that you engage each level of your management team in your transformation journey, because they play a critical role in building a new culture. Include them in establishing priorities and determining action plans, and hold them accountable for achieving these priorities. Don't allow them to revert back to their technical comfort zones. Be sure to position your people for success by investing in them and providing them with the new skills and tools they'll need to be successful. This approach will help you address today's priorities while building momentum toward the future.

Warning! Do not start down this path unless you are seriously committed to sustaining it. If your transformation efforts are not continued, you will add to the cynicism level created by past transformation attempts that ended prematurely or were pushed aside by yet another flavor of the month. Slow and steady can win the race, but starting and stopping is not an option, as it will negatively impact your reputation and the credibility of IT across the enterprise.

So, let me modify the statement I made at the very beginning of this chapter. I still say there's never been a better time to be in IT, but I'll add that there's also never been a more challenging time in IT's short history. The question is, are you up for that challenge? Because if you are, we at O&A wish you nothing but success and are excited that you have included us in your transformation journey!

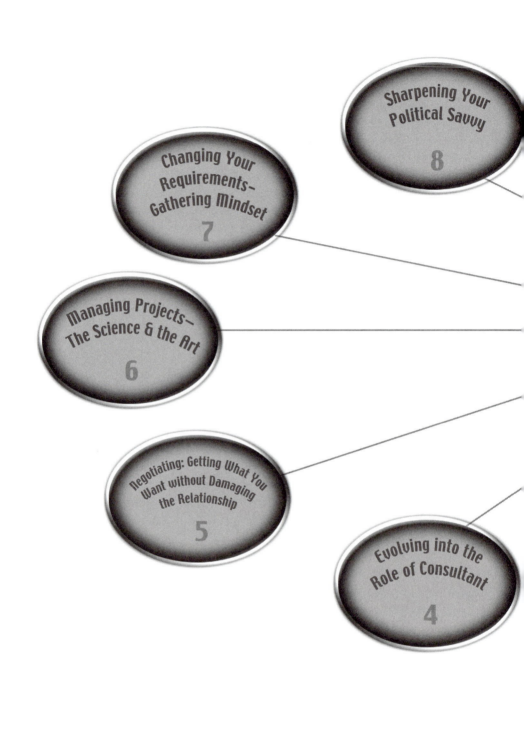

Sharpening Your
Political Savvy

8

Changing Your
Requirements-
Gathering Mindset

7

Managing Projects-
The Science & the Art

6

Negotiating: Getting What You
Want without Damaging
the Relationship

5

Evolving into the
Role of Consultant

4

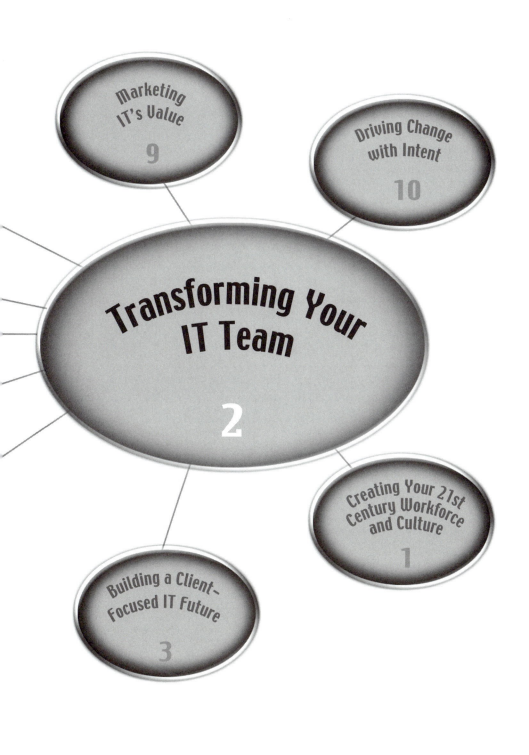

I t's relatively easy – when you're on the outside looking in – to see when an industry or profession is in the midst of a revolutionary transformation. Journalists, for instance, are currently facing identity crises as people flock to blogs for news and insights. The entertainment industry continues to evolve, as younger audiences spend more time with reality TV programs and amateur videos on the Web than with situation comedies on TV.

It's more difficult to have this perspective when it's your own profession that's undergoing radical change. But that's exactly what's happening in IT. In my nearly 30 years in corporate America – including 18 years in internal IT (five as a CIO) and four as an external consultant – I've seen the demands placed on IT leaders change from keeping the mainframes humming to leading high-performance organizations that partner with the business to consistently deliver successful solutions.

Many IT professionals are still evolving toward that role. But the fact is, IT leaders have no choice but to transform themselves and the organizations they lead. Today, business leaders require CIOs and other IT leaders not only to exercise exceptional leadership behaviors, but also to lead their teams in sustaining strong client partnerships, demonstrating business and financial acuity, executing successful projects and delivering exceptional results.

And this transformation is hard work – it's threatening, humbling and draining. It involves research, retooling and missteps all along the way. This is especially true for the people I've seen promoted to the highest IT ranks based more on their technical prowess than their leadership capabilities. And often, these are the people who don't fully understand the need not only to undergo such a transformation themselves, but also to lead their IT groups to become high-performance organizations, as well. No wonder the average tenure of a CIO or CTO these days is just two to three years!

But as painful as this transformation might be, it's a necessary change for IT professionals who want a successful future in technology for themselves and the departments they lead.

I first got my feet wet in leading team transformations about 15 years ago, when I was working at a Fortune 500 company and found myself continually being put into positions to help turn departments around. My approach was a commonsense one; in each case, I'd see what was broken and develop a plan to fix it.

As I saw each area reach its full potential and the positive impact that had on people's lives, I became even more motivated to fine-tune my skills to affect a faster turnaround the next time. It's so great to see people actually enjoy what they're doing! The positive energy is magnetic. Those experiences were a turning point for me, and I now consider that time as my "boot camp days" of learning about effective team transformation.

During that time, I developed what I call my "recipe" for transforming departments and teams. The best thing about it is that anyone with the right mindset can follow it. The recipe involves assessing your team's strengths and weaknesses through external feedback, developing a plan to overcome weaknesses, choosing a handful of top priorities, promoting the success stories and then refreshing that plan every six months after you determine what's working and what's not. Even if you're not in a blatant turnaround situation, it's my firm belief that no matter how well your team is operating, there's always room to raise the bar.

"Who, me?" I've heard many an IT leader say. "I don't have time to change, and I don't see the need to." And that may be true. But just to be sure, it's important to take a look inward. When I talk with IT leaders, I urge them to heed the following warning signs that signal a change is necessary:

- Client and executive dissatisfaction with IT performance and outcomes.

- Strained client relationships.

- Too many No. 1 priorities.

- Missed IT goals, objectives and metrics.

- Inability to effectively position and sell IT ideas and solutions.

- Missed project deadlines, budgets and client-expected outcomes.

- Talent shortfalls – absence of IT consultative, financial, project leadership and business-savvy competencies and skills.

- IT silos inhibiting teamwork, synchronization of efforts and bi-directional communication.

- IT resource constraint issues.

- Unclear IT roles and responsibilities.

- Inability to achieve agility, flexibility and scalability.

- Excessive system downtimes.

- Difficulty in negotiating airtight vendor contracts and effectively managing vendor performance and results.

- The perception of IT as commodity resources rather than competitive advantage enablers that deliver undisputed value.

If any of these conditions sound familiar to you, then I urge you to start developing the mindsets and strategies that are necessary to be a high-performance leader. These mindsets have less to do with programming and system architectures and more to do with interpersonal skills, business knowledge, communication, critical thinking and decision-making.

And it's not just about transforming yourself – you need to build a culture of leadership throughout the IT organization. I've never met a successful IT leader who also didn't have a great leadership team. In fact, when I was interviewing for the CIO position I held for five years, I wrote down a list of ideas of what I would do if I were hired. Eight months into the job, I came across that piece of paper and had to laugh – all those ideas had been accomplished! But it wasn't all by me – it was due to the leadership team I'd put in place and the environment I'd created in which people could reach their full potential.

It's a basic tenet of IT leadership: You simply can't be effective if you don't foster a great team. Whether you've got a team of 500, 1,000 or two, you can only perform as well as the weakest link. Unfortunately, I don't see a lot of collaborative teamwork happening in most IT organizations. Instead, I see territorial, silo-oriented attitudes toward resources, responsibilities and budgets. I see people focused on their functional areas and rarely ever taking the enterprise view. IT organizations have to wake up to the fact that none of us "owns" anything – it all belongs to the enterprise.

The entire IT organization needs to behave like a surgical team, where everyone knows what needs to happen next and collaborates with precision. And just as a nurse seamlessly hands off equipment to the surgeon, IT professionals need to just as effectively complete their own hand-offs. In IT's case, that means reflexively asking questions like, "Who else will this impact?" "Who else should be involved?" "What resources do I need?" and "Who do I need to talk to?" And once those questions are answered, it means following through with effective communication and ensuring the hand-off occurs. When this kind of collaboration occurs, no ball ever gets dropped!

Collaboration has to be encouraged at the highest levels of the enterprise, and rewards for teamwork have to be built into performance assessments. IT professionals need to know they're being measured based on their contribution to the greater good, not their own (or their team's) individual performance.

The cold, harsh truth is that technology executives who continue to ignore the need to transform themselves and their teams eventually become organizational casualties. But if you choose to embark on the road to high-performance leadership – and work with your people to impart the same competencies – your organization will be a force to be reckoned with.

SECTION 1

How to Make This Transition: Learn to Think Differently

It's so easy to fall into old, comfortable habits. But as I work with IT leadership teams across the country, I find there are six mindset and behavioral changes that must precede a successful leadership transformation:

MINDSET CHANGE 1:
FORCE YOURSELF TO PLAN AND THINK OF THE BIG PICTURE

Like it or not, IT can no longer afford to be all things to all people. Given all the demands for technology-enabled business initiatives, it's actually beneficial to everyone – including your clients – to develop a strategy that's based on a set of clear, finite priorities formed by what's most important to the client, both within IT and out in the business. That way, if clients ask for systems or projects that are off the list, you can help them see for themselves where these requests fit in (or don't fit in) to the overall business strategy. When someone tries to add something to our plates, you can manage that situation effectively rather than running around fighting fires.

I often hear IT leaders say, "I could be more strategic if I just had more people to get things done." But it's a vicious cycle – without a strategy, you'll never have enough people, because it's impossible to "get it all done." The only way to line up your resources effectively is to identify priorities based on business strategy. In some cases, I've seen organizations discover they have extra resources, which enables them to volunteer for additional projects – doing wonders for their reputations.

The important thing is to have a collective, consolidated view of what IT needs to get done. And that view needs to extend across the entire organization – I've seen leaders make the mistake of letting each IT area identify its own list of priorities that eventually conflict with each other. Instead, the entire IT organization needs to develop one set of priorities, all focused on what's most important to the business.

Developing this list of priorities depends, of course, on getting out there and talking with clients on a frequent basis. IT leaders need to venture out into the business community and interact with peers and department heads on a formal and informal basis, and they need to encourage their staffs to mingle with their business clients, as well. This is so important that we've covered the topic of networking and building rapport in great depth in Chapter 4.

In some cases, when you meet with business leaders, you may discover that they don't yet have a clear strategic plan themselves. But you absolutely can't take that as an excuse to not move forward. In fact, if you've established a strong level of trust as an IT leader, you're in a great position to encourage business leaders to develop a strategy and even facilitate the process of building one. They would come around quickly if you can articulate to them that without a strategy, there's no way to establish priorities, and without priorities, there's no way to assign resources to achieve the outcome they expect. People generally respond when they see the "win" in it for themselves.

Of course, this conversation can't even take place if you don't have a prior relationship with business leaders. So for some of us, the first step is identifying the people you need to develop a relationship with, whether in IT or in your client base, and then reaching out to them before you need something from them. It has to be genuine.

MINDSET CHANGE 2:
ADOPT A PROACTIVE APPROACH

You simply can't be a leader if you assume a passive, victim's mentality. I see too many IT organizations that would rather point fingers, cast blame and take the easy way out. But true leaders create the future, and that means doing the hard work of assessing the world around you and taking preemptive action. It may seem at first to be a much harder path to take, but it's ultimately much more satisfying to realize we can take actions that will affect the outcomes in our lives.

I've seen dysfunctional leaders, who wait until they hear a critical mass of client complaints before they take steps to improve their department's level of service. Or they assume everything's going well because – rather than interacting with staff, clients and fellow executives who could provide them with critical input – they're more comfortable sitting in their offices answering e-mail.

High-performance leaders, on the other hand, are always looking to raise the bar, before clients complain. They're socially aware, able to read the political landscape and engage in social networks. Indeed, effective leaders spend much of their time working with people, including clients, other leaders and their staff. They also make it part of their staff's performance reviews to report on what they've done to nurture their key relationships.

MINDSET CHANGE 3:
RESIST THE TEMPTATION TO DELVE INTO TACTICS

Many IT leaders are techies at heart. They love jumping in and fighting fires when crises arise; in fact, they may even believe that no one else on their staff could resolve the problem as well as they can. Plus, it's fun being the hero, and it's definitely thrilling to rise to a demanding, immediate challenge.

However, it's not your job as an IT leader to react to short-term situations; you need to be strategizing about the future. If you don't do it, who else will?

In my leadership workshops, I consistently hear participants say they don't have time to engage in leadership activities. One told me he didn't have time for the "soft and fuzzy stuff" involved with building relationships. I tell these people there's something very wrong going on if that's the case. Perhaps they don't have an effective team in place, or perhaps they haven't created an environment in which the team knows what's expected of them and are accountable for their performance.

Others use "no time" as an excuse for the fact that they hate pulling themselves out of technology work. They don't like solving problems that involve people; they'd rather work with technology, which is more cut and dry. If that's the case, a leadership position may just not be for them.

Very often, leaders would have the time if they managed their time better. It's amazing how terrible our time management skills can be, even at the highest positions in the company. For instance, e-mail can be a real time-suck – it's all too easy to be drawn in by every new e-mail that crosses your screen. I recommend that leaders check it three times per day – once in the morning, once at noon and once at night – and otherwise shut it off. Meetings are another one. I recommend creating agendas for our meetings and sticking to them. If you develop agendas in advance, people can be prepared, and meetings will progress more quickly and smoothly.

Becoming less tactical and more strategic also requires quiet time, so schedule some "think time" on your calendar. It's easy to let your calendar get filled by meetings – including meaningless ones, like vendor lunches – but you need to have the discipline to schedule time for strategic thinking, which might mean leaving the office and going somewhere off-site where you can find peace and quiet.

I know a CIO at a global company who visits client sites around the world to talk with them about their needs. When he returns, he schedules time on his calendar to review his notes and follow up with suggestions and strategies to fulfill those needs.

Delegation is another crucial tool for clearing time on your schedule. This, of course, requires having staffers who you trust to lead in your place. As CIO, I used to have customers call me and ask that I, personally, get involved with something they wanted done. Even in those cases, I would sometimes delegate the work to a trusted staff member. I'd assure the client that they were in good hands and that I'd hand-chosen the best person for their needs. It's all how you position it.

If you feel you're the only one who can jump in when problems arise, that's a warning sign. We may love being the hero and revel in resolving crises, but those are reactive activities, and we're consigned to be proactive leaders.

It's easy to think we don't have the time to do this leadership work, but the fact is, that's why we were hired; it's the value we bring. We need to take a close look at what we do with our time and clear the decks of non-value-add tasks by delegating to our staffs, managing our time more effectively and analyzing whether certain tasks are even necessary.

MINDSET CHANGE 4:
BE CANDID WITH YOURSELF AND OTHERS

The best leaders I've seen have the courage to be candid, particularly when it comes to conflict. Generally, people don't like conflict and seek to avoid it, mainly because they don't know how to deal with it. Navigated well, however, conflict can actually be part of a very constructive process that ultimately leads to innovation. That means keeping emotions out of it and not taking disagreement personally. If there's something you don't think is working, say so. It's a coward's choice to verbally agree and then walk away full of resentment that you didn't get your way. Dealing with conflict is such an important skill that we've covered the topic of conflict management in Chapter 5, where we focus on learning to negotiate.

Another place where IT leaders need to be honest and candid is with their own capabilities and weaknesses. When you're candid about your weaknesses, you can surround yourself with people who are strong in those areas. And when you take this self-assessment, it's important to identify real areas of weakness, not superficial ones. Maybe you're weak at selling ideas, overloading your schedule, getting impatient with people, losing your temper. Maybe you have trouble developing relationships, motivating or coaching direct reports, delegating responsibility, being positive, or maybe you're shy. Once you identify such challenges, you can begin to work on them or hire people who can fill in the gaps.

MINDSET CHANGE 5:
PREPARE FOR AND EMBRACE CHANGE

The IT profession is all about change. And if you as an IT leader resist change or never see it coming, it can have a truly negative impact on the company and on your career. If you act like the ostrich with its head in the sand, choosing to ignore change, you'll miss the opportunity to effectively manage the expectations of the business, your clients and your staff.

Change comes in many forms. There can be changes in corporate culture, business direction, industry competition, or in technology direction. There can be disruptions in the geographic landscape or changes to government regulations, legal requirements, and security threats.

Whatever the flavor of change, we need to be aware of its potential and be capable of analyzing how to deal with it. One good way to do that is to apply the "SWOT" tool – identifying the strengths, weaknesses, opportunities and threats of the change. This topic is so strategic that we've dedicated Chapter 10 to developing the ability to lead change.

MINDSET CHANGE 6:
ANTICIPATE, UNDERSTAND, RESPECT AND WORK THROUGH
COMPLEXITIES

There's no getting around the fact that our success depends on our relationships with our clients, peers and staff. Effective leaders absolutely
must get out of their offices and from behind their computers and work
on developing relationships. It's only by frequently talking with clients,
staff and peers that you can anticipate what's coming down the road,
develop a mature understanding of how that affects key constituents and
gain the trust of the people you work with to respectfully work through
those changes and complexities.

You might even consider developing a relationship strategy. At one company I consulted with, IT leaders worked to identify five or six key people
they needed to develop relationships with, whether they were clients
or members of the executive team. From there, they could move on to
another group of people, developing relationships in a genuine, unforced
manner.

SECTION 2

Five Critical Success Factors that Enable IT Organizational Excellence

Changing your own mindset is one thing. Leading your IT organization
through a successful transformation is quite another. In my work with
technology leaders around the country, I've determined that there are five
challenges leaders need to work through when they want to re-position
themselves and their organizations for success.

1. LEADERSHIP:
LEAD BY POSITIVELY INFLUENCING AND INSPIRING OTHERS

The exceptional technology leaders I've seen have an inner quality that
makes other people want to follow them. That means learning to influence and persuade others by sharpening interpersonal skills and communication techniques. It requires building trusting relationships that
enhance our ability to get things done through other people. And it also
requires becoming resilient as you learn ways to increase your energy
and effectiveness under pressure. Building these skills is so important

Maximize Your Strategy, People and Operations Investments

that we've covered them in more depth in Chapter 4 on consulting skills, Chapter 5 on negotiating and Chapter 8 on political savvy.

2. STRATEGY:
ESTABLISH THE RIGHT WINNING "GAME PLAN" FOR YOUR ORGANIZATION

The second challenge is developing a transformation strategy for your organization to follow. A well-constructed, thorough blueprint is the first step to setting the stage for IT success. In fact, a solid game plan is essential to increasing profitability and competitive advantage, driving down expenses, maximizing productivity, strengthening customer service, optimizing people potential and protecting client, investor and company data.

What if you were planning to take a cross-country car trip – would you just get in the car and drive, or would you develop the best plan to get you there? Would you think you were doing well just to drive really fast, or would you want to be sure you were headed in the right direction? It's amazing that we plan our car trips better than we plan our IT activities! Remember: activity does not equal progress. We need to develop a strategy for getting from here to there, one that works for everyone involved with the plan.

I like to think of strategy as a river, with many different tributaries feeding into it. Each tributary represents something that eventually helps build the ultimate plan, whether it's marketing the IT organization, continuously improving performance, optimizing human capital, understanding the business needs and putting together the technology architecture. We need to work on each of these building blocks in order to develop a strong overall plan.

Too often, I see strategies that are so nebulous that there's nothing concrete or actionable for anyone to grab hold of. Other times, they're complex, 500-page binders that collect dust on a shelf. Still other times, I see a strategy that's well constructed but hasn't been communicated effectively. Just recently, I visited a company at which the IT leader had developed a strategy but hadn't clearly communicated it to the leadership team. When I asked them to explain their strategy, they just looked at the floor!

So, what should the strategy look like? It should be simple, no longer than a 12-page document, with some graphics that clearly display the strategy focus and the plans to make it come to fruition. And it shouldn't just sit on a shelf – strategies need to be reviewed and refreshed (although not necessarily rewritten) every three to six months because things change. It's a living, breathing document that needs to be communicated across the organization so people understand where exactly they plug in.

At my workshops, I advise IT leaders to communicate their strategy in many different ways, including face-to-face, formal gatherings and informal small-group forums. I also encourage them to avoid devising unachievable or intangible targets driven by generic ideals and "blue sky" thinking. Too often, I've seen IT groups discard fuzzy visions that they disdain as "flavor of the day" management.

Strategy is also not built in a vacuum. It's vitally important to identify and involve key constituents, particularly those who will provide the business perspective. Most important, we can't let the strategy focus exclusively on technology selection.

Once the strategy is established, we can articulate and prioritize our activities. Remember, it's always better to execute on a few activities and see success rather than bite off too many things and execute poorly.

3. PEOPLE:
HIRE AND PROFESSIONALLY DEVELOP YOUR WINNING TEAM

The third challenge is to form the team who will work together to execute the strategy. I've never seen a strong leader who operated alone. Our staffs and leadership teams are our lifeblood to achieving success. That's why CIOs, CTOs and anyone in charge of an IT team also needs to learn how to select, coach, develop and optimize their staffs.

One of the worst mistakes I see happening in IT organizations is the short-circuiting of the interview process, where questions are superficial, and employees are hired based merely on "chemistry." Quick hiring decisions often result in the selection of the wrong person, which can lead to lost productivity, increased costs, missed performance targets or poor employee morale. A surprising number of companies do a horrible job of checking references, even though the best predictor of future behavior is past behavior. When I've checked references, I've always gotten great information. You just have to come across as personable, professional and willing to help out the reference, should they also need anything in the future.

As leaders, we need to know how to assess who on our staffs – or from outside the organization – has the right competencies and capabilities to execute the strategy and then develop plans to help these people grow and professionally develop.

Training efforts should be aimed at the right people, taking into consideration how each employee will immediately leverage it, how it will be integrated into daily work and how the results will be measured. We also need to retain our highest performers and develop succession plans in case a top performer leaves the company.

Strong performance measurement also comes into play, especially to measure how well the leadership team fosters a culture of collaboration among their teams. For instance, how well do they support their peers? What have they done to develop genuine relationships with key stakeholders? How well are they hiring, retaining and developing their own staffs?

When I was hired as CIO, the first thing I did was throw down the gauntlet to the leadership team and told them they'd have to break down the silos among their areas, work out the adversarial relationships that existed and operate as a cohesive team. I made it clear that as leaders, they were responsible for sitting down together – without me as an arbitrator (we're all adults, after all) and negotiating a game plan in which the enterprise itself was the winner. I made it clear that no personal agendas were allowed – we would do what was best for the business, period. Thereafter, everyone in the organization knew they had no choice but to play well with each other. I tolerated no "we vs. them" stuff.

Breaking down these silos and rewarding teamwork and collaboration takes a great deal of work and leadership to accomplish, but it is absolutely essential. But most organizations are not structured this way – it's more often a culture of "every man for himself." It looks like a bunch of people who jumped into a rowboat, started rowing in all different directions and ended up going around in circles. The fact is, we're all in the same boat, and to make any progress at all, we all have to row in the same direction. And the top IT leader is 1,000% responsible for that because only he or she can set the tone.

In summary, leaders need to do the following, when it comes to hiring and professional development:

- Instill leadership competencies and behaviors.

- Select people with the right skills and experiences that align with the position qualifications to execute the technology strategy.

- Build leadership bench strength.

- Embrace performance measurement and best practice methodologies that shape behaviors into desired results.

- Learn how to select the right employees the first time.

- Identify professional development programs that deliver sustainable results through phased-in learning, accountability mechanisms and coaching.

- Recognize that employee interpersonal competency and skill development is mandatory.

4. Best Practices:
Leverage IT Best Practices Right-Sized for Your Organization

Once you've got the right people in place, it's time to start thinking about execution. But before you do that, you need to become current with the best practices in your area of focus (commonly found in the Fortune 500), select the ones that are right for your organization and then resize them to fit your company's structure, culture, complexity, strategies, goals and business and technology drivers. Even small- and medium-size companies can benefit from right-sizing the best practices of larger organizations.

Best practices are a fundamental cornerstone of any technology strategy. After all, why re-invent the wheel when there are time-tested, established approaches that achieve great results every time? Best practices also help us break out of the pattern of "doing things the same way we've always done them."

Of course, it's also important to avoid the dangers of best practices, such as creating a highly complex, cumbersome process that kills organizational agility, stifles innovation and creativity and destroys customer service. Best practices can't be taken off the shelf and used without customizing them to our own company culture. I always advise companies not to use anything more complex than what the situation calls for; as a great CIO I know once said, "If a client wants simple directions to the store around the corner, don't give them an elaborate map showing them how to get to the North Pole."

You also have to be careful to adopt best practices that truly match the challenges you're trying to solve, not the ones that look good because of all the buzz and hype around them. Use what makes sense for your organization and for your end goal. I see too many IT organizations apply best practices without stopping to ask, "What's the problem we're trying to solve, and what do we need to do about it?"

Done right, best practices can apply to all facets of our IT organizations, including strategy, talent, finance, operations, systems/applications development, customer relationships, third-party relationships and communications components. Some best practice programs include:

- Business and Technology Plan Alignment

- Client Relationship Management

- Business Needs Assessment

- Performance Scorecards and Measurements

- Portfolio Management

- Project Management Office

- Risk Management

- Organization Change Management

- Business Case Development

- Selective Outsourcing

- Problem and Change Management

- Service Level Management

- Financial Management

- Vendor Management

5. EXECUTION:
TRANSLATE YOUR STRATEGY, GOALS AND INITIATIVES INTO SPECIFIC ACTION PLANS THAT DELIVER MEASURABLE RESULTS.

The final challenge – execution – is where the real action begins. Or it's supposed to, anyway. In actuality, this is where many IT leaders drop the ball. What I find is that IT leaders regularly underestimate what's required to reach the end goal. They don't step back and look at all the moving parts and complexities, put together a game plan that addresses the top priorities, implement the mechanisms to be sure the game plan takes root and then measure the results to ensure the end goal was achieved.

Surprisingly, many IT leaders seem to think all they have to do is say, "We're going to go do 'X,'" and it will get done. Without a real execution plan in place, they don't realize that 'X' will simply wither on the vine. Eventually another priority will come along – let's call it 'Y' – and suddenly everyone shifts over to working on Y and abandons X until it's just another forgotten initiative.

At some companies, this happens often enough that the IT organization learns to regard new strategies as "flavor of the day" that after a bit of lip service will fizzle out. They learn to simply ignore any new initiative that comes along. At a company I was consulting with, a staffer once said to me, "There's no way this new strategy will ever happen, so I'm just going to bide my time for a few months until it goes away."

That's why I advise IT leaders to run their transformation initiatives like they would any other project, where they assign a project manager, form project teams, develop project plans, create reporting mechanisms and measure results. It's amazing how many organizations shudder at that thought! One client told me it's because they wanted their transformation initiative to be regarded as "fun," and projects were decidedly not seen that way. I pointed out to them that you can create elements of the transformation that are fun but that on the whole, leadership work is tough. You need structure, and you need people who are committed to driving the changes into the fabric of the organization's culture.

I've seen IT leaders who simply can't do this kind of transformation work because they don't want to make unpopular decisions. They're not willing to make the choices to make the transformation work become reality. They just want to be regarded as a "nice guy." But part of being a leader is making those tough decisions. And your staff will thank you for it. It's like raising kids – they'll always test the boundaries, but in the end, they operate better when they know where the boundaries are.

Execution is not a simple thing. It involves translating strategies, goals and initiatives into action plans, project plans and individual performance plans. You need to plan the work, empower your people, balance strategy with tactics, capture key performance indicators, track performance progress, adjust to changing conditions, measure the results and apply "lessons learned" to strengthen future execution precision.

All along the way, it's vital to have the right tools in place to be sure people are executing on the work. This requires having a set of measurements, using a balanced scorecard approach, based on the results clients want to see. The whole goal is to see the project through the client's eyes and ensure you're capturing the right set of measurements from the client's perspective.

But the key word is "results" – too many times, IT organizations think things are going well when there's lots of activity. Well, it has to be the right activity, aimed at achieving the right results. Customers are mainly interested in speed, low cost, expected outcomes and a good overall experience, and high-performance organizations will deliver on all four of those components.

CONCLUSION: HIGH-PERFORMANCE REALITY

Leadership is a journey, not a destination. IT leaders need to continually raise the bar, working relentlessly to develop themselves and their staffs to improve their leadership qualities. I've seen organizations take years to do this when they start from scratch, but I've also seen others make quantum leaps in very short periods of time because they were hungry and prepared for the change.

If developing and executing an IT transformation were easy, every IT organization would be doing it. But enduring such a change is absolutely essential to distinguishing yourself from a dying breed. IT leaders simply aren't what they used to be, and choosing complacency is like choosing to be the frog in a pot of water that's gradually being brought to a boil. If you don't want to become a casualty, you better not sit around.

We've all observed people in other industries turn a blind eye to changes that are clearly making them obsolete. Now that the spotlight is on IT, it's time to adjust your own vision and see your way to a needed transformation.

Top **10**

Leadership Strategies for Transforming Your IT Team

10. Prioritize time investment to deliver optimal results.

9. Build solid client relationships and strategies.

8. Effectively navigate politics and executive team dynamics.

7. Keep abreast of technology and business trends.

6. Think strategically while balancing tactics.

5. Align with the business.

4. Focus on results.

3. Keep promises.

2. Be resilient and effective under pressure.

1. Build trusting relationships.

SPECIFIC ACTIONS I WILL TAKE

✔

✔

✔

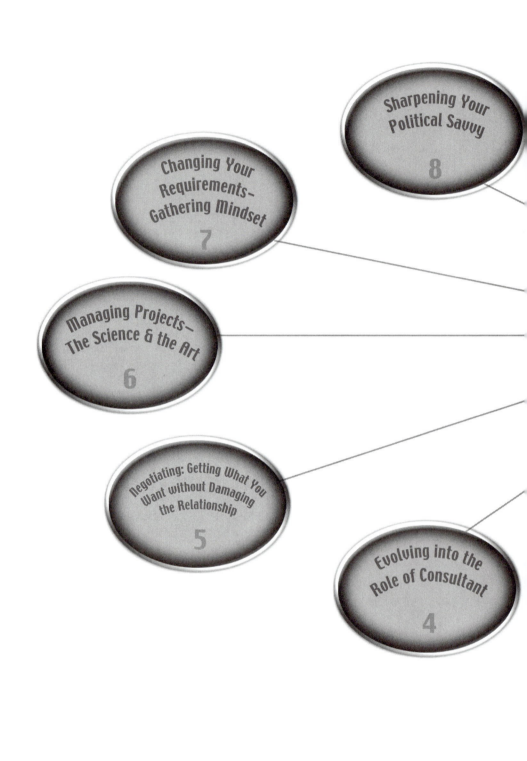

Sharpening Your
Political Savvy

8

Changing Your
Requirements–
Gathering Mindset

7

Managing Projects–
The Science & the Art

6

Negotiating: Getting What You
Want without Damaging
the Relationship

5

Evolving into the
Role of Consultant

4

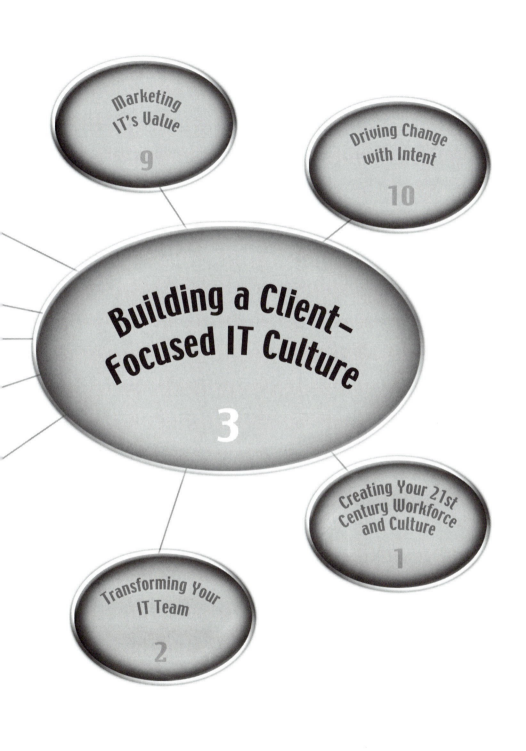

Marketing
IT's Value

9

Driving Change
with Intent

10

Building a Client-
Focused IT Culture

3

Creating Your 21st
Century Workforce
and Culture

1

Transforming Your
IT Team

2

When you hear the term "good service," what springs to mind? Dinner at a four-star restaurant? Flying first class? Staying at a luxury hotel? But when you think about what separates these elevated experiences from the more mundane (a rushed lunch at a diner, a middle seat on an overcrowded plane), it's not all about the imported food, the $10,000 mattress or the extra elbowroom. There's an essential ingredient that must accompany that free glass of champagne before you'll be satisfied, and that ingredient is called service.

But how do you define good service? At an abstract level, it's the sense that the people involved with the transaction are fully engaged with meeting the expectations you have regarding the experience they're providing. For instance, the surroundings are clean and well-decorated, your needs are met promptly and courteously, you're treated with respect, and if you ask for something that's not within the usual range of offerings, the staff works to accommodate you the best it can.

Less abstractedly, it's the waiter who checks on your order even though he's not assigned to your table. It's the hotel receptionist who offers you food and beverage credits if the reservation system neglected to honor your request for a non-smoking room. It can even be the retail clerk who looks you in the eye and asks – in a manner that suggests he truly cares about your response – whether you want to bring home your purchases in a paper or plastic bag.

Notice we've left the luxury environment at this point. Just because you expect to receive this type of service when you're paying a premium, that doesn't mean it's impossible to find four-star service at any convenience mart or roadside hotel. And just think what happens when you do encounter good service in these commodity-level places – if you later have a choice of which hotel to frequent, you'll very likely return to the one that not only rented you a room but was also engaged in the experience of bringing you satisfaction as a customer.

Now think about the characteristics of good service as it pertains to the work your own IT team does every day, maintaining, supporting and building technology systems to enable clients to carry out business initiatives. Are downtime and upgrades planned at times that are most convenient for your clients – or for the IT organization? When a client approaches someone in the IT organization with a request, does the individual tell the client it's not their area, or does he or she look up the name of the person who can best help the client and then walk them to that person's cubicle? Or when a client explains a problem to the help desk, do they get a gruff, "What operating system are you on," or a reassuring, "I'm sure we can get that resolved – why don't we start with what operating system you're running?"

From what I've seen as an internal consultant with Unisys and Cannon and during my 15 years as a consultant with O&A, being a service provider is a new idea for many IT professionals. A remark I often hear from people who participate in the workshops I facilitate on this topic is, "Isn't WHAT we deliver more important than HOW we deliver it?" But for anyone who feels this way, it's time to think about their job and their career in a different light.

The fact is, I've watched IT leaders and staff make and break their reputations with service missteps, thinking that their client base is secure and has nowhere else to go. An even bigger fallacy that I've witnessed is the belief that if the outcome of the work is good, it doesn't matter how difficult you were to work with. As a result, IT is unappreciated and undervalued and seemingly blind to the minor (and major) service irritants that trip up their reputations.

To me, it's an absolute shame that many of the smartest, hardest working and logical members of any company are so unappreciated and undervalued. It's imperative that understanding IT's role as a service provider (not servant!) is essential to IT getting to the table and being heard as a true and valued partner.

Because whether your staff believes it or not, the best way to build client loyalty is not by proving IT's technology prowess but by building a service strategy that enables internal IT to be seen as a top provider of service. In fact, a well-developed and well-communicated service strategy is critical in today's IT organizations. Clients demand service to be immediate and proactive, and if they don't get it internally, they'll find it, either by hiring their own staff or external vendors. Indeed, good service is no longer just a nice-to-have; it's the make-or-break factor that determines whether clients choose internal IT or someone else to deliver the solutions they need.

In too many IT organizations that I encounter, a good service strategy means "being all things to all people." But while everyone is equal in the eyes of the U.S. Constitution, not everyone is equal from a service perspective. In others, the service strategy seems to be to provide service only to the people who scream the loudest and have the most clout. This leads to a tremendous amount of frustration on the part of IT, as well as the clients who don't have that same level of clout.

I also see IT organizations that have created service strategies that are interwoven with their governance practices, where a committee makes decisions about what's best for the organization at large. This strategy can be great, but I notice a lot of confusion both among the business community and the IT staff about how this strategy actually operates. That's usually because this strategy requires lots of communication as to how decisions are made, especially since the lag time between meetings can be months.

But most of the time, I see no strategy at all, or even well-thought-out strategies that haven't been communicated well to those providing the service. Having a clear communication plan is the key.

For all of these reasons, the development of a service strategy has to start at the top of the IT organization – with the IT leader. These strategies require cultivation and have to be planned and led by the IT leadership team. The strategy has to be consistent across the enterprise, and it must permeate every project, not be something that "only Joe" provides. After all, good service is not defined by good relationships with individual clients. The purpose is to look out for the enterprise, not make "my friend in accounting" happy.

At its best, service is a mentality, an attitude, glue that holds together the entire department. And it can't spring from a negative environment. The turn-around can be difficult, and it can be costly, but it can also turn your internal IT group into a must-have resource for clients.

Section 1
What Good Service Looks Like

Let's start by talking about what service doesn't look like. Number one, service is not subservience. It's not about becoming submissive order takers who deliver anything the client desires. But while IT can't do everything the client asks for, it can convey a willingness to serve, and it does this by addressing the client's needs with respect and concern. If you've succeeded, the client walks away from the transaction, thinking, "I really like working with these people."

Service also can't spring from a negative atmosphere. Unfortunately, many IT departments are hotbeds of negativity. I hear IT professionals complain about feeling unappreciated, angry, victimized. "We're always called in at the last minute," is a frequent comment, or, "All the decisions are already made by the business," or, "We're invited to the party after all the food is gone." In other cases, I detect a note of arrogance – "They couldn't survive a day without us," or, "It's always up to us to save their skins."

No wonder when some IT leaders ask their staff to up their service game, they might glumly play a role that they think looks like good service but isn't. It's the mentality of the store checkout clerk who asks without expression or eye contact whether we found everything OK or the false smile of the flight attendant who tells us to have a good day. If there's one thing about good service, it only passes the sniff test when it's sincere.

So what does good service look like from an IT point of view? Some characteristics include:

- Sincerity.

- Righting wrongs instead of abdicating responsibility.

- Addressing issues promptly and courteously.

- Working to understand the client's needs.

- Going out of your way to resolve an issue.

- Being easy to work with.

- Approaching issues constructively.

Above all, service starts with understanding – and really caring about – the client's goals and concerns. This requires a change of attitude, from negative to positive, and to thinking of the client's concerns as imperative to IT's function, not something that gets in the way. Sometimes it's easiest for me to convey what this change of mindset looks like by showing some examples:

- Instead of listing all the reasons IT can't support something, how about listing what the organization can support that might meet the need? (Of course, that involves asking what the client's need is in the first place.)

- Instead of telling clients that the changes they're requesting will throw the project off budget and off schedule, how about laying out the impacts and asking what's most important to the client?

- When a server goes down or the client isn't able to access a particular application, how about an apology for the impact to his/her job?

- How about telling clients that you're thinking about them and their business, for instance by sending them a note of congratulations when they win a large project or finish something for the company?

In my workshops, I also like to point out the two most common wrong-doings I see committed in IT today when it comes to service, as well as how to correct them. These two "service sins" happen when people play the roles of either the Rule Master or the Promiser. The Rule Master says things like, "That's not part of the project plan," or "that's not our company standard," or, "we don't do it that way," or, "that's not our policy."

On the other hand, the Promiser just says "yes." "We can do that," "We can do that too," and, "Is there anything else you want us to do?"

Both roles are played with the best of intentions – the Rule Master's is to manage expectations and protect the company, while the Promiser's is to build good relationships. The best way to stop these common practices is by taking those best intentions and getting them pointed in the right direction.

For instance, with the Rule Master, hold a staff meeting and ask your team what rules they're most often asked to break. You'll likely hear things like, circumventing the process, starting work without funding or approval, giving access rights to unauthorized individuals, providing support for clients' home devices. Then, as a team, discuss what your reply should be to each one. The reply should focus on what IT can do to help or better understand the root problem the client needs help with.

And if there's a rule that clients continuously challenge, that gives you two pieces of information. First, maybe it's time to get rid of this rule. If not, maybe it's time to address this rule at a communication level, so everyone understands the business rationale behind it. Again, as leaders, we must make sure we're not giving exceptions to the rules simply because it's uncomfortable.

With the Promiser role, it's important to understand that saying yes makes everyone happy at first, but if you can't deliver on that "yes," it's the disappointment and anger that will be remembered. So, first IT needs to understand what situations cause them to over-promise. Second, you need to plan some phrases that show your concern, prove you're knowledgeable and that give you a chance to truly listen and understand before committing to anything. For example, you might say, "I know you're asking us for a delivery date, as this change is really important to you. But given that importance, we want to make sure we can commit to the date so that you're pleased at the end of the project and not just now. Let's keep talking about what you need and then give us a half-day to get back to you with a commitment."

If the meeting is virtual, having a signal or key word can help team members understand when someone has begun to over-commit.

SECTION 2
Service Skills and Mindsets

In order to transition their organizations to a service-oriented culture, IT leaders need to help all members of the IT staff develop a new mindset. Here are three skills I teach in my workshops to evolve participants' mindset toward a service-oriented culture.

1. A "WE" MINDSET

Developing a service mentality is not an individual effort. It's a team sport, where things like a good pass, an assist or runs-batted-in are more important than achieving a "personal best." In other words, think football, basketball and baseball, not golf, track or swimming. A superstar is always fun to watch, but the more the team depends solely on that player's performance, the less chances it has of winning.

The "we" mentality is important on many levels. The first is within the IT team itself. All too often, people in the IT department take each other for granted, treating each other as though they don't count as much as other co-workers do. But imagine what the IT group would look like if its members saw each other as deserving of a prescribed level of service. Not only would group members work together in a more fluid, respectful and effective way, but also good intra-department service is essential for providing good service outward, to business clients. If there's negativity within the IT organization itself, it will surely be evident to the business community.

The team mentality is also important because a service-oriented culture requires that clients experience consistency across all members of the IT team. In other words, no matter which individual a client works with, he or she needs to experience the same positive attitude. If some team members are friendly and engaged while others are angry and negative, clients will simply avoid the unpleasant individuals and seek out the constructive ones. At one health organization I worked with, clients regularly avoided asking for help on the days when they knew a particular IT professional was assigned to help them.

Consistency is important for another reason – developing loyalty among business clients. Imagine you're taking a road trip, on which you'll need to make a couple of overnight stops before reaching your destination. At your most road-weary, you pull into the parking lot of a brand-name hotel, where in the past, you've learned to expect a certain level of service. You expect to park close to the hotel door, walk into a clean lobby, easily get a room that meets your needs, take a swim in an attractive pool, get a simple dinner at a nearby restaurant and sleep in a comfortable bed.

Now, what would happen if the brand-name hotel you chose didn't meet those expectations? What if the staff never brought the extra towels you requested, the receptionist couldn't recommend a good family restaurant, and no one was available to make more coffee at the free breakfast buffet? As you grumpily drove off after such a poor-quality experience, would you choose that brand of hotel at the next stop? It would help if the low service level was an anomaly, but at the very least, it would reduce your enthusiasm for using that brand again.

Similarly, clients will more quickly increase their loyalty to internal IT when each and every experience they have with IT team members is a positive one. It's an unfortunate fact that negative experiences have much more impact than positive ones.

A "we" attitude is also important when it comes to the IT organization's relationship with its clients. Too often, IT develops an "us" vs. "them" mentality toward the business, which suggests a separation at best and a combative relationship at worst. To shift toward a service-oriented culture, that us versus them gap must be closed. IT organizations must realize that they and the business are part of the same whole, that the very reason they want to provide excellent service is that they're working with their business counterparts together to achieve common organizational goals.

At one company, this destructive mentality was so strong that the IT group had started a "Stupid User Award" at their monthly staff meeting, where they'd vote on the stupidest thing a user had done that month. While there's nothing wrong with blowing off some steam, institutionalizing and emphasizing such a superior attitude was not going to help this group develop a service mentality. When they realized this, the group turned the award around, voting instead on the smartest thing they'd noticed a user doing that month.

This us versus them mentality can also creep in when IT professionals mistakenly interpret the service provider role to be that of an order taker. If you can picture yourself pulling out an order pad and taking down requirements without understanding what the client wants and why, you need to stop what you're doing and get engaged. Internal IT and the business client are both part of the same community that has a vested interested in doing the best job for the company, and there's no room for us versus them; there's only room for "we."

2. LEARNING TO LOVE COMPLAINTS

This is one of the harder mindsets to develop. Who could love a complaint, whether it's in the form of a neighbor who can't stand your dog barking or a threatening letter from the bank? Well, what if you stripped the emotion out of the complaints you hear and simply saw them as input or information that you otherwise wouldn't be privy to? Don't you want to know that your dog barks for an hour as soon as you leave the house? Or, that your check bounced? If you didn't hear the complaint, how else would you be able to take action before something worse happened?

IT needs to learn to love comments like, "What were you people thinking when you chose this standard?" "Will you ever accomplish anything on time?" "I like you, but that other group in IT, the business analysts, they're very arrogant." "You know we call it the Help-less desk, don't you?" "It's been two months since I put in that request. How come I can track my package with UPS but you folks manage to lose things?"

The IT organization needs to know that its standard hasn't been well received or well communicated. It needs to know that a peer group has an arrogant reputation (and so do they)! It needs to know the help desk hasn't been given the tools that they need to properly help callers. It needs to know that somehow a request has been neglected.

As an IT professional, it should be much more disconcerting to NOT hear your clients complaining – all too often, unhappy clients remain quiet, giving you no chance to prove you can do better. And bad news does have a way of spreading more quickly than good news. For better or worse, complaints are often your clients' form of communication, and not only should you treasure them, but you should also encourage them. Complaints are a learning opportunity, your opportunity to get it right. You can't do something with what you don't know.

In some ways, complaints are comparable to the problems IT works on every day. What's often missing is the process of resolving them. Unlike a system glitch – which gets tracked, trended and reported on – you may not know what to do with a complaint. That's what makes it so crucial to harness complaints and address them via a complaint management process. If complaints are addressed quickly, courteously and effectively, imagine the percent of the complainers who will come back to you with their future needs.

But first you have to interpret complaints correctly, which means listening for the problem being expressed. This isn't always easy. Complaints often sound disrespectful, or even hostile. But as soon as you look beyond the personal dig and turn complaints into something that's trackable, logical, non-personal and non-emotional, they're easier to deal with. That means overcoming IT's natural defensiveness – "Technology changes overnight; we're lucky we can keep up with it," "You think you've got problems?" Or even a tendency to agree in non-constructive ways – "Yeah, I know, the situation really stinks," or "Yes, our policies really are archaic." What message do those responses send?

IT organizations need to develop a new way of responding, which most people aren't trained to do. A workable process might look like this.

Step 1: Thank the client for making the complaint. It sounds counter-intuitive, but this step really helps to force a mindset change. A simple, "Thank you for letting us know" will do, and you might even want to add a little marketing twist: "It wasn't our intention to make the process seem slow."

Step 2: Gather more information. You need to help your staff get past defensiveness and start asking questions to find out more about the problem. Make sure their line of questioning is open-ended and designed to let the client tell his side of the events. The goal is to investigate, not interrogate. The attitude should be, "Tell me what's wrong, how did it happen, how can I better understand the situation?"

Step 3: Apologize for the circumstances. Even if you don't think it was IT's fault, you can express this as, "It wasn't our intention to interrupt your business process," or "I'm very sorry you had that experience."

Step 4: Ask how you can help. This doesn't mean pulling out the order-taker pad or putting on your "I'll-fix-everything" hat. This step requires really listening to all the circumstances of what happened and what the client is unhappy about and coming away with a commitment to taking measures that rectify the situation.

It's all too easy to cut the conversation short and ask the client to send an email, detailing his complaint. But it's crucial to take the time to follow these four steps when the client is in front of us, willing to talk. And it's just as crucial that when the conversation ends, the client feels a commitment has been made to resolve the problem to his or her full satisfaction.

Note that resolution and satisfaction don't always mean making the client happy. For instance, if someone complained that the company wasn't moving more quickly toward a new computing platform, you can't snap your fingers and make the budget appear to do that. However, you can ask the client to flesh out his concerns and ask how you can help him feel more comfortable with the pace of new technology adoption. Maybe you can share the schedule of when the new platform will be adopted, as well as your thoughts on why it's smart to hold out for that timeframe.

Again, the "how" is just as important as the "what" – and that includes the tone and manner in which you communicate. Even if it feels like you've addressed the same complaint a dozen times that day, you need to avoid sounding like you'd really just like the client to go away. When IT professionals start to feel like their jobs would be so much better if their clients would just leave them alone, that's when you know you're heading down the wrong path. Because the result might be exactly along those lines – the clients will indeed leave you alone, as they make their arrangements with the new technology provider.

And none of this is easy to do when emotions are high. At one hospital I worked with, the IT group had taken down the pharmacy system over the weekend for maintenance, without warning the people who depended on it 24x7. On Monday morning, when they walked in to irate clients, it was hard for the group to not feel completely discouraged. But because of their progress toward incorporating a service-oriented mentality, they were able to turn that attitude around to realize that through the mistake, they learned valuable lessons. They thanked the clients for detailing their complaints, ensured them of their commitment to rectify the situation and were able to move on. Through their service mentality, they gained an opportunity to recover from a bad situation.

3. MAKING EVERY INTERACTION COUNT

The third mindset focuses on the daily interactions IT has with its clients (both business clients and IT peers) and recognizing that every impression counts when it comes to providing good service. I call these "moments of truth" – interactions that leave our clients with an impression of IT's performance, whether positive or negative. The term "moments of truth" was conceptualized in 1984 by service management guru Richard Normann and later popularized by Jan Carlzon, a renowned business leader and turnaround specialist, who wrote a book by that title.

In the average IT organization, hundreds or thousands of these "moments of truth" occur every day. Clients form impressions every time they encounter the IT group, from the first voice they hear when calling the help desk, to the first link they click on IT's Web site, to the first person they see when they enter the IT group's area of the building or campus.

Moments of truth can work to IT's benefit or detriment. While one negative experience can cause the client's impression to sour, it takes just one positive interaction to begin repairing a negative experience. If you map out the service you provide into moments of truth, you can start to understand how clients experience the internal IT group and start making micro-improvements that can have a huge impact.

Consider what happens when a business department becomes interested in off-the-shelf software it can use to help it better communicate with the company's suppliers. The client talks to the vendor, and in doing so, experiences the following moments of truth: The vendor compliments the client, tells them they're ahead of the game, gives them a demo showing all the great things this product can do for the organization, leaves behind a good-looking brochure and provides an estimate within the promised week.

Then the client talks to internal IT. In this case, the moments of truth can go one of two ways. In the first, IT reacts positively, saying, "Yes, we've heard about this product, and we'd love to sit down and hear your goals for what it can do for you." IT then compliments the client for their savviness in the technical area (only if it's true of course) and promises to provide an estimate within the week. In the other scenario, IT could tell the client it has too many projects going on right now to deal with the client's request. IT then tells the client it can't even research the system until it assigns a project or task number and ends the conversation with a noncommittal, "We'll get back to you."

Notice that I haven't even begun talking about the moments of truth involved with refining requirements, testing, going live and support. Each of these stages can have hundreds of moments of truth, involving different clients who are part of that same organization.

Consider the moments of truth involved when IT sends out an email, announcing it needs to perform a system upgrade. Moments of truth can include: who the email is from, what's in the subject line, what does this mean to me, when will this occur, can I opt out of this. If the upgrade involves turning in a laptop or PDA for a new, better one, moments of truth can include: what does the device look like, is all my old stuff on it, what has been removed, what has been added, where is that certain function I like, how long is this going to take, can I reschedule? Then the client needs to figure out how to be productive again. Here, moments of truth include: did this technology actually improve my work, and when I call for support, is the staff knowledgeable, or were they just trying to get up to speed on it themselves?

When you have virtual clients, moments of truth are a bit more challenging to manage. First, these clients expect a quick reply to their calls, emails or instant messages, just as non-virtual clients do. If the staff isn't available during certain hours, expectations need to be managed via out-of-office features on email and via updated voicemail announcements. Second, because it can be easy to lose touch with virtual clients, you need to make sure your top 10 clients are contacted by phone at least once per month. Third, it's also easy to lose track of how changes in the home office affect virtual clients. This boils down to more communication by IT regarding the changes that affect these clients.

Moments of truth can also be less formalized, like interactions with clients we pass in the hallway. If someone stops to give an IT staffer his or her idea for a new enhancement to an application, does the staff person look the client in the eye? How does he or she react – with a sarcastic, "Great, another new idea," or with a positive, "Those are the kinds of suggestions we're always looking for." Even non-verbal reactions count, including facial expressions, eye contact and tone. All of these have long-lasting impressions.

Remember, attitude is everything. Does your staff turn requirements-gathering meetings into grill sessions, or are they enthusiastically engaged in the discussion? These are all the ways in which clients measure the IT organization.

If you map out all the moments of truth that clients experience with the IT organization and assess what their experience is like through those interactions, you'll have a good idea of your organization's level of service and where it needs to improve. This can range from voice tone and body language to a grander scale, like revamping all your forms or streamlining your Web interface.

The Service Strategy Cycle

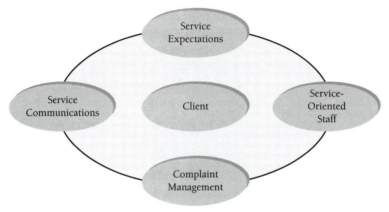

SECTION 3:

Strategies for Developing a Service Mentality

At any point in time, an individual IT professional can decide to change his or her own approach to providing service – whether by adopting new body language or tone of voice or even the way they respond to client complaints. However, the real call to action is for the entire IT department to undergo a cultural shift. It's up to the IT leader to not only acknowledge that it's crucial to craft a service strategy, but to also communicate the strategy and be sure it's used consistently by all members of the IT staff. Here are some tips for making a service strategy work:

1. NEVER LET IT GO

IT leaders who want to affect a service mentality culture talk about the issue all the time. At every meeting, no matter how technical, they convey the sense that the client is at the center of the discussion, or they make the connection between how the technology issues intertwine with the business. One company that had traditionally incorporated a "safety moment" into every monthly meeting, in which the IT group discussed one thing it had done to improve its alignment with OSHA standards, also began incorporating a "customer service moment," in which it reported on measures taken to better serve customers.

IT leaders also need to encourage individuals to understand what their clients are working on, what the business is doing and what the stress points are. This can be done quite easily through many tools that most companies already offer, such as internal newsletters and Web sites that many people in IT may not think to read. It doesn't need to be time consuming; skimming through the information or just looking at the table of contents can yield valuable insights.

Another way to conquer the time commitment conundrum is to take a divide-and-conquer approach. For instance, I've seen some companies assign various IT team members to read business journals or books pertaining to the company's industry and make a 30-minute presentation on what they learned at a monthly meeting. The same idea could be applied to "field trips" into the various client areas that IT serves, whether it's the manufacturing line, the reservation system or the marketing area.

It's surprisingly easy to forget about making clients the center of your everyday life. At one think-tank organization, the CIO got so wrapped up in managing budgets, reorganizations, internal staff and meetings that he realized one day that it had been two years since he'd last talked with any of the IT department's clients. He certainly wasn't shirking his job duties; he simply lost sight of the fact that anything the group was doing was for the sake of the client.

A challenge we frequently hear is that while individual leaders within the organization "get it", in terms of having and conveying a service mentality, other leaders don't and actually do harm. While this can be very discouraging, it's all about perseverance. Those of us who do "get it" need to continue reminding our peers about the impact we have on determining IT's reputation. Research shows that peer pressure works well in changing others' behavior. So the best thing you can do to influence other IT leaders throughout the organization is to continue reminding them of the importance of a service mentality and initiating small steps, such as the ones mentioned in this chapter to show your commitment and stay positive. Make it a mental game if necessary.

2. CLEARLY DEFINE YOUR SERVICE LEVEL OFFERINGS

With compressed budgets and time schedules, the days are gone when IT can or even should offer the same level of service to all of its clients or even assign the same service level to all areas of IT. It's more strategic to define several levels of service and decide how to apply those levels based on the needs of your clients.

For instance, you might define three levels of service:

Basic: Focus on quick turnaround.

Enhanced: Focus on quick turnaround and client convenience.

Premium: Focus on all of the above plus anything else that's required, as long as the client is willing and able to pay for it.

Note that all three levels are quality offerings; what changes, is the amount of time that IT dedicates to the issue. For instance, a client that's launching a new product that's critical to the bottom line would require premium levels of service, as would an executive traveling overseas to make an important presentation. On the other hand, a non-revenue-producing group might be assigned basic service and given a lot of self-service tools.

You might also expect different levels of service from different areas of IT. The help desk might be considered a basic service, where the attention is on quick turnaround, whereas technology R&D is an enhanced service that has the added requirement of hosting a Web site on its findings.

No matter how many levels of service a company defines and how it applies them, it's crucial for individual team members to move easily between the various levels. It's equally important for clients to know what to expect. Retailers do a good job in this respect. Think of what you expect when you walk into a store like Nordstrom's vs. Costco. Shoppers would be incensed about waiting in line at the former, but they're mentally prepared for that at Costco. A service motto can go a long way toward helping to avoid the guesswork of what service clients should expect and what IT is required to give them.

The big secret to managing expectations is the ability to understand what the client's expectations are in the first place. That might sound really obvious, but IT organizations are often afraid to ask this question, because they're concerned they won't meet it. However, it's impossible to meet an expectation that's unknown.

After understanding the client's expectations, the next step is to stop focusing on what you can't do and gear your mind to what you can do. Say a client asks you to install some non-standard software. You can't do that, but you can offer to load and support the approved standard. If clients are complaining about a late rollout, a positive response would be, "I'd be happy to call our R&D folks and find out where we are on testing this product and give you status on when the rollout will be." If someone asks you to change a spec on a project you're in the middle of, say, "We'd love to make that change for you, but of course, every change has an impact on the schedule or the cost. Would you like me to get those numbers for you?"

There seems to be an awkwardness (almost an embarrassment) when IT manages expectations. However, I like to remind people I work with that clients are very used to this behavior from external vendors!

3. Engage Your Clients in the Culture Shift

A service strategy will only be successful if your staff sees things through the eyes of the client. A great way to provide your organization with that vision is to invite clients into the process. You can ask them to share their impressions of IT service, for instance, or even attend a workshop together. Some of the participants in my workshops have invited key clients to attend with them. In either case, a face-to-face dialogue is much more revealing than a written survey.

Depending on your relationship with the client, this can be a painful but eye-opening experience. For instance, one manufacturer that had what it described as a "broken" relationship between the business and IT attended one of my workshops. A top business client frankly detailed his group's impressions of IT, many of which were negative. The revelations ranged from "We don't hear from you," to, "We don't know what you're working on," to, "You're always having these big reorganizations," to, "When we call you, it takes you forever to respond." The message: We're in the dark, and when we do need you, we can't find you.

It wasn't easy to hear, but by the end of the day, while the relationship was by no means completely mended, it was on its way to being repaired. On IT's side, this was no time to be defensive; it was time to be quiet and listen. And on the client's side, it was not so much about blame as investing the time and passion to reveal some difficult truths. In the end, it's far better for IT to hear these assessments than for the client to share them with someone else.

CONCLUSION

Management fads come and go, but a service-oriented mentality is no blip on the screen. It requires leadership to affect culture change from the top down, and it requires every member of the IT team to become engaged in a new mentality of delivering technology services.

Furthermore, developing a service strategy is a process, not an end result. With every day, every moment, every interaction clients have with IT, impressions are formed, for better or worse. Customer satisfaction surveys are great, but it would be wrong to focus solely on increasing your score each year. The true goal is to satisfy clients every time you interact with them.

So what do we get for providing good service? The sad fact is, there's often no immediate reward. Good service is expected; it's poor service that gets noticed. But, even if IT doesn't get credit, good service is long, long remembered, and those memories come back to benefit IT in the form of client loyalty. So when it comes time to decide between internal IT and another technology provider, it's service that will raise your IT department above commodity status.

It's important to remember that internal IT is no longer the only game in town, and the days are gone when clients depended solely on IT to provide technology services. There are other ways for clients to fulfill their technology needs, and service is a competitive part of the equation in determining which provider to use – internal or external IT.

But there is great hope here! Behaviors such as loving complaints (rather than arguing why you're right), understanding the organization and its goals, and watching the attitude of, "that's against policy" can lead to enormous good will from clients and allow IT to actually get credit for their phenomenal work.

If you live each day of your work life knowing it can all be taken away by an external vendor in a heartbeat, that would be the beginning of a shift toward the mentality and motivation needed to redefine your IT organization as a provider not of technology but of service.

Top 10

Ways to Build a Client-Focused IT Culture

10. Identify and avoid the service sins you commit when under pressure.

9. Document who your clients are, as well as which services you provide to them.

8. Define the levels of service you are willing and able to provide.

7. Elicit feedback on the levels of service you choose to provide.

6. Clarify problems *before* you start fixing them.

5. Know what your clients' expectations are *before* trying to meet them.

4. Learn something new about one of your clients (goals, hot buttons, concerns).

3. If the service you provide is virtual, spend more time thinking about and creating touch points (Web sites, voicemail boxes) than if you were on-site.

2. Ask clients for feedback on one self-service tool (or try it out yourself).

1. Talk to a client and ask, "What is your biggest frustration with IT?" "What is the best thing IT does?

SPECIFIC ACTIONS I WILL TAKE

✔

✔

✔

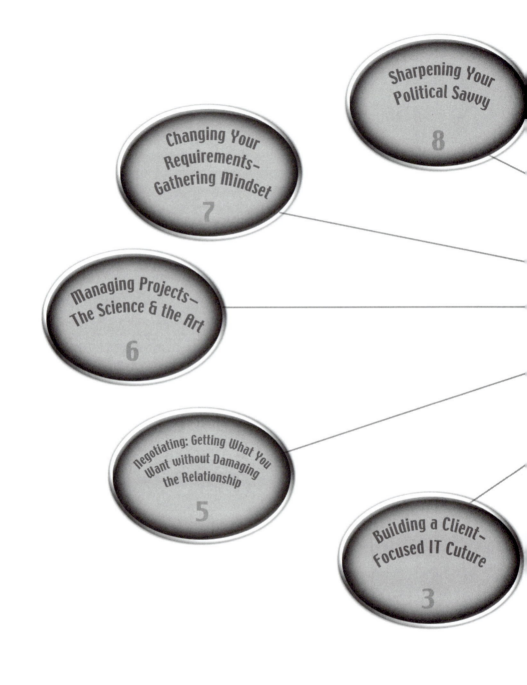

Sharpening Your
Political Savvy

8

Changing Your
Requirements-
Gathering Mindset

7

Managing Projects-
The Science & the Art

6

Negotiating: Getting What You
Want without Damaging
the Relationship

5

Building a Client-
Focused IT Cuture

3

Marketing
IT's Value

9

Driving Change
with Intent

10

Evolving into the
Role of Consultant

4

Creating Your 21st
Century Workforce
and Culture

1

Transforming Your
IT Team

2

Throughout life, people face big decisions that are outside their usual realm of expertise – how to pay for their kids' schooling, where to buy a house, which medical procedure is best for addressing a health concern. At those times, many of us reach out to someone with more knowledge than we have, whether it's a financial planner, a realtor, a doctor.

Think of the qualities you look for in the person you ultimately want to engage with: Expertise, certainly, but you might also want someone who really listens, who takes the time to understand your desires, concerns and goals, who can explain things in a way you understand and whom you can trust to have your best interests in mind.

What you're looking for is a consultant, someone with whom you can enter into a partnership that allows you to enrich your own perspective with his or her experience. It would be foolish to try to embark on really complex and important decisions or projects without the help of such a person.

My 25 years of experience in consulting with and for organizations has shown that unfortunately, that's not what happens in corporate America every day, when it comes to making important technology investments. When business departments embark on new strategies or seek better ways of doing their jobs, they almost always require technology expertise to reach those goals. But to whom do they turn for that expertise? Time and time again, across every industry I've consulted in, I've seen them seek out an outside consultant, a technology vendor, or a power user in the department who knows enough to be dangerous. But who ultimately needs to implement the solution? The internal IT department – often when it's so far down the road in the decision-making process that the system is difficult or even impossible to implement in a satisfactory way, given the current infrastructure and architecture of existing systems.

And after too many project failures, some business departments end up sidestepping the IT department all together. And how dysfunctional is that? It's like trying to build a house and avoiding contact with the general contractor.

In some cases, I've seen business departments enlist the help of IT earlier in the game, but with the expectation that their system specifications will be carried out without discussion or costly involvement of their staff. IT obliges, and when the system ultimately doesn't do what the client really needs it to do, everyone starts blaming each other and the system falls into disuse.

In fact, this is the situation that most resonates in the workshops I facilitate for O&A on consulting skills. One of the biggest complaints I hear from IT professionals is that they can't get their clients intimately involved in the project because they lack availability or sometimes even interest. For me, this is a clear indicator that the client is not fully owning the outcome, and that doesn't make sense, given that it's rare for any project to be an IT project – rather, it needs to be a business project.

Consider this scenario. When a Minnesota couple needed to transfer to Florida, they faxed their home requirements to a Florida realtor. The realtor called back and suggested a phone conference. The couple was annoyed; why couldn't the realtor just work with their specifications? But by the end of the conversation, they learned how much they didn't know about housing in the South. In fact, had the realtor delivered on what they'd asked for, they would have ended up with terrible buyer's remorse. In the end, they bought something they never would have considered if they hadn't engaged in the consultation – but that was ultimately the right house for them.

The lesson for IT leaders is this: Clients of computer technology are a lot like that relocating couple and like anyone who needs to get something done that's beyond their realm of expertise. We think we know what we want – a college education, a dream house, a clean bill of health – but if a trusted and learned partner doesn't help influence our decision-making, we may very well end up dissatisfied. In the same way, your clients may think they know what they want, but too often, "what they want" doesn't jibe with the reality of how technology actually works, or with existing architectures or in tandem with other systems.

In my consulting career, I've always been intrigued by what it takes to manage the dynamic forces of people, processes and technology in order to create business solutions. In fact, my interest led me to pursue a master's degree in organizational development, in order to better understand the human side of getting work done. Then, over the years as both an internal and external consultant, I started to recognize that the IT organization's success in bringing business solutions to fruition often came down to its ability to *influence without direct power*. And that's why today, I find great satisfaction in working with IT professionals to support their own development as internal consultants. I strongly believe that their effectiveness in partnering with the business is directly correlated with the development of their personal interaction skills.

I also believe it's crucial for IT leaders to enable themselves and their organizations to engage clients in a trusted partnership, shifting their role from "order taker" or "technology wizard" or even "naysayer" or "bottleneck" to the role of "problem-solving partner." By operating as a consultant to the business department, IT professionals and their clients are putting their capabilities together to build an optimum solution with which both sides are happy.

SECTION 1

What Exactly Is a Consultant's Role, Anyway?

Many IT professionals have probably never really thought about what the word "consultant" means, and if they have, it's usually based on a negative stereotype they have of external consultants. But in fact, from the CIO down to entry-level staff members, everyone in the IT organization needs to expand their influence by operating as a consultant. So, let's get past the negative connotations and think of what a consultant really is – someone who has no direct authority or power over the people he or she works with but instead uses influence to guide their decisions and actions. In other words, since consultants don't operate from a position of authority, they have to operate from a position of trust – trust not only in their expertise but also in their ability to share that expertise in a meaningful and applicable way with their clients.

This is true for everyone in IT, not just people with the word "consultant" in his or her title, and not just for client-facing positions. After all, the minute the CIO walks out of her office and into the business community, she has lost all her positional power and is only as good as her ability to influence her peers and clients. Today's reality is that the success of the IT professional absolutely hinges on earning the trust of our clients. Otherwise, why would they listen to us?

Perhaps it's easier to understand the consultant role by envisioning what it is NOT. Consultants are not the gurus at the top of the mountain, to whom clients make pilgrimages and pay homage. They are on the ground, side-by-side with the client – an ally who is fully engaged with the business needs at hand.

Imagine a patron walking into a restaurant – he's hungry but not sure what to eat, so he asks the cook to just make him something delicious. Forty-five minutes pass, and the diner's annoyance turns to outrage when the meal finally arrives, and it's a casserole containing all sorts of vegetables that he doesn't like, sausage – which he doesn't eat – all swimming in a tomato-based sauce – and he hates tomatoes! How could his request for "something delicious" have gone so wrong? The customer sends it back, only to anger the cook, who had labored over this meal, imagining that it would send the diner into epicurean ecstasy.

Have you ever experienced that type of frustration? Like when you've agreed to insert yet another requirement into a system that's already behind schedule, only to have the client berate you a short time later when a deliverable isn't met?

Now imagine that the cook had asked the diner a few questions, like whether he's allergic to any foods, what else he'd eaten that day, whether he prefers seafood or red meat, how much he wants to spend or whether he's ever tried parsnips before. As the cook engages the diner more fully and gains a stronger understanding of his preferences, he might steer the customer away from the dinner menu and suggest something from the luncheon menu, which can be prepared more quickly.

Just as important, the cook doesn't make the customer feel stupid when he needs to explain why it's impossible to prepare potatoes au gratin without adding cheese or why the diner probably shouldn't order a soufflé for takeout. He also doesn't waste the diner's time explaining which cooking implements he'll use, what the optimal food temperatures would be or whether he prefers to brown the meat before roasting it. And if anything happens during the meal preparation to change the discussed outcome, he'll make sure the customer is quickly made aware of it.

Although all of this front-end work takes time, it's worth it: While awaiting his food, the customer is well prepared for what he's going to get. And when the meal arrives, he's not only completely satisfied, but he also vows to return to this restaurant because he's developed a real rapport with the cook.

That's the type of trusting relationship IT leaders need to develop with their business clients. In this type of true partnership, you're not blindly following orders or bluntly saying, 'No, that can't be done' without discussing alternatives. When there's trust and real effort put into understanding the needs at hand, both the IT professional and the client can discuss, negotiate, push back, give in – all without feeling like someone needs to win or lose. Because suddenly, it's not a battle anymore.

So how do you get there? It requires IT leaders to develop a whole new mindset, as well as a set of skills to help clients define what they really need, within the constraints of budget, schedule and what's technologically feasible. When IT organizations do this, I've seen them transform from the people called in at the last minute to the go-to-group that business clients call as soon as they consider a new system need. Just like they would with a trusted consultant.

Here, generally, are the characteristics that clients expect to see in a consultant:

- Confidence in his or her own capabilities without arrogance.

- Enthusiasm and complete engagement during the project.

- Accessibility and responsiveness.

- Knowledge about the client's line of business and a willingness to learn more.

- Dedication to the client's best interests.

SECTION 2:
Why Do I Need to Become More Consultative?

Some people ask me whether it's truly vital for IT professionals to develop their consulting skills. Isn't it more important to keep up to date with certifications and technology skills, they ask? I respond by reminding them that it's not about "either/or" but rather "and." As a good consultant you need to bring value to the table. That means you bring technological perspective in respect to the business AND you have the human interaction skills so that people will actually be able to hear what you have to say.

Over the years, I've had many IT professionals confess to me that they were resistant to this "touchy/feely" stuff until they tried it and evolved into a consultant role. When they do, it represents a major shift in their thinking. In fact, many will confide that they wish they'd been a little wiser much earlier in their career.

That's because in the past decade, information technology has become so intertwined with business strategy that the one can't – or shouldn't – be pursued without the other. IT professionals who are more excited about technology than its application to business initiatives will increasingly find themselves working on non-strategic, non-core and ultimately not very exciting projects – if they continue to be employed at all.

In my work with a major retailer, I had one of the senior business sponsors announce to a new group of IT staff members, "I get really nervous when someone from IT comes in and says, 'I have a great idea!' because I get the feeling they're probably excited about some new technology advancement. But when they come in and say they have an idea on how we can accomplish some business goal or objective – I'm all ears. I need people who are committed to helping me drive the business agenda – not the latest and greatest technology."

IT is under increased pressure to deliver technology solutions more quickly and cost-effectively and to quantify the return on investment.

How better to accomplish that than to pair technology projects so closely with client needs that no one could question whether any given technology project is bringing value? And how better to reduce costs than to deliver what clients really need the first time, rather than abandoning expensive efforts and going back to the drawing board time and time again? The only way to do that is to foster the relationships that enable understanding and collaboration.

Lastly, competition has never been hotter for internal IT, particularly as lower-cost offshore options are becoming a more familiar and often-used choice for low-level coding and routine testing and sometimes even more strategic projects. As one IT executive said to me recently, "I'd have my head in the sand if I didn't realize the competition is out there." Today's IT department also functions as the resource broker or the general contractor on key projects. It is their role to find the right mix of employees and onshore/offshore resources. By operating as internal consultants, the IT organization can avoid being replaced by outsourcers.

SECTION 3
Learning to Change Hats: The Four Roles of IT

In my workshops, I refer to four different consulting roles: Technical Wizard, Technical Assistant, Silent Influencer and Problem-Solving Partner. All have intrinsic value when used at the right time. Here's a quick description of each:

- The **Technical Wizard** is the hero role. They descend upon a problem with all their wizardry and save the day. You need heroes on your team, especially when there is a crisis. However, the Technical Wizard doesn't necessarily help build a shared understanding or commitment for the long term. Some clients would love nothing more than to let IT take charge with no involvement and then blame IT when it doesn't address the real need.

- The **Technical Assistant** can appear as the *order taker*. The business department knows – or seems to know – exactly what it wants, and IT carries out the stated requirements. However, sometimes taking the order is not the right solution. This role can result in clients getting what they ask for, but not always what they need. Their requests are not informed by the realities of what it takes to fulfill them, and IT doesn't truly understand the business situation in which the client is operating.

- **Silent Influencers** are actually not silent but informally influence their clients' perspectives. For instance, you can send clients articles on relevant topics or hold brown-bag lunch gatherings to explain technology concepts and how they relate to current business needs. You can even just check in with clients via phone or e-mail to see how things are going with existing business initiatives or ongoing projects. In some organizations, I've found this to be one of the most effective roles to gain greater ownership and in-depth understanding of the technology solutions. One of my clients, for example, reported great success from merely stopping by his key client's office weekly. He said his client's perception was that customer service had improved over the last few months. It's amazing what a little personal attention can do. In today's environment, our clients are often geographically dispersed, requiring more creativity to stay in touch. Technology does enable us to communicate, but resorting back to voice communications may provide even more relational contact. For example, one IT leader I've worked with schedules regular coffee breaks on the phone, essentially 15-minute check-ins to see how things are going with her clients. Remember, if you're not influencing your client, someone else is.

- The opportunity to have the greatest influence is to step fully into the **Problem Solving Partner** role. The analogy that I use for this role is that you and your client are getting into the same car to navigate a road trip. You decide together where you're going and how you're going to get there. You both bring valuable perspectives that need to be considered along the way. When you encounter an unexpected problem, there's no blaming. You reassess your options and proceed. When the journey is over, you celebrate your accomplishments and share the lessons learned for the next trip.

This last role is one that appears to take more time. But my experience has shown that the upfront time involved pays you in dividends at the back end because you get the job done right the first time. For projects that are complex and involve a host of sponsors, you can't afford not to have everyone in the car when you begin the journey.

The technical wizard and technical assistant are often the roles in which the IT department builds a solid reputation. When your business clients have confidence in your ability to deliver value, they will be receptive to your role as silent influencer or problem-solving partner.

SECTION 4:

So, How Do I Become a Consultant?

For most IT organizations, transitioning into the role of "consultant" requires a fundamental shift in approach and mindset, as well as the development of a new set of skills. Historically, technology expertise may have gotten you hired, but today, it's business acumen that gets you invited to the table, and it's human interaction capabilities that will get you invited back.

Today, I find more and more examples of individuals being hired because of their business savvy, and they're taught the technology skills needed. Clients will have confidence in you if you know where to go to obtain in-depth technology knowledge, as long as you fully understand the business realities.

In some cases, IT even hires for personal interaction skills. I know of one CIO who five years ago stopped hiring programmers to get the technology skills he needed on-staff. Instead, he began hiring people who were strong in interpersonal skills and then sent them to the local community college to gain technology skills. His goal was to create a team that could create a strong connection with the business. And hands-down, he tells me, these are the programmers that the rest of the organization consistently requests to be on their project teams.

At the same time, it's important for IT leaders to create a spreadsheet of its technology competencies and weaknesses. There needs to be a plan to be sure resources are there to meet future needs, whether in the form of outside experts or bulking up training efforts. It's simply impossible for everyone on the team to stay current with his or her skills, with technology changing at today's current pace. Today's IT leader is responsible for determining the best mix of resources, both internal and external.

Let's take a closer look at the business and communication skills that IT leaders and their staffs need to develop to become more consultative. It starts with IT professionals taking full responsibility for the messages they communicate and the impact it has on others.

BUSINESS ACUMEN

When it comes to developing business acumen, the goal is to educate yourself and your staff on the clients' areas of expertise and the current business pressures they face. How do you do this? Mainly by spending time with clients, watching how they interact with existing technology in their day-to-day work life and asking good questions when they're approached for a technology change or new system. You and your staff need to become students of the business and learn enough to speak the client's language and understand their real issues.

This requires developing good interview skills. For instance, before launching into a new project, IT professionals should ask clients what issues they're trying to resolve, what they're trying to accomplish and why that's such a concern for the business. During this conversation, you need to work to identify the root problem the client is having – you may find the client doesn't need a new system at all but a feature that's already available in an existing application or that could be built through a simple modification. We cover interview skills in more depth in Chapter 7 on gathering business requirements.

Or it could be the opposite – the client may think it's a simple request to just add another column to a spreadsheet, without understanding that this request involves accessing data from another database. In the end, it might be better to solve the issue manually and use IT resources for something with higher payback.

It's only by understanding the business environment as well as the challenges, responsibilities and pressures that clients face that IT can apply technology in the most effective way possible.

HUMAN INTERACTION SKILLS

Perhaps even more important, most IT professionals also need to strengthen their communication skills in order to interact with clients effectively. While left-brained skills such as analytical thinking, logical reasoning and sequential capabilities are important for the systems-building side of the job, consulting requires right-brained skills such as listening, empathy and dealing with emotions.

Here are some of the more important human interaction skills IT leaders and their staffs need to develop.

AUDIENCE PROFILE

Few IT departments have the luxury of starting from scratch in building a relationship with their clients. There's usually some history, either positive or negative. One important skill is learning to develop an audience profile. Who exactly is your client? Identify what you know, what will impact the project, the client's tech savvy and the past history with IT. Do your business clients trust the IT department and have confidence in its capabilities, or is there some repair work that needs to be done?

Clearly, you'd use a different strategy to influence a client who's on-board and enthusiastic about getting a new initiative started vs. one who feels he or she has been burned in previous systems projects. You can't just leave that elephant standing in the room. But remember, once you start talking about the elephant, it's important to hear out the client's grievances without becoming defensive, even if you think they're completely wrong. It's important to acknowledge any issues in your organization's history with the client and lay out a plan to regain their trust.

LISTENING

You might think of listening as a passive activity . But good listening actually requires a lot of work if you want to ensure that you understand what you hear, absorb it and act on it with any degree of accuracy.

Active listeners aren't silent during the exchange; rather they clarify what they hear, paraphrase what they think they understand and ensure that they're not making incorrect assumptions. We all filter what we hear, either adding extra details or skipping over points that we deem unimportant but that may be crucial.

Indeed, incorrect assumptions are the bane of any listener. Even seemingly simple words can mean vastly different things to different people. What would you think if a client says he needs to see a system in 20 days – that he wants to be up and running with reporting capabilities in that short timeframe? Or that he wants to see a plan or a high-level design? It's not unlike the classic cartoon portraying a client asking for a swing, and different developers picture everything from a tire swing to an executive chair hanging from a tree. You need to clarify, paraphrase, and play back the speaker's words to ensure you have an accurate understanding.

I like to illustrate this in my workshops with the following exercise: I ask one person to relay an event that takes around 60 seconds to tell. Then I ask someone who was listening to retell the story as accurately as they can. The re-teller is almost always surprised by the extra details they add and the pieces they leave out because of the assumptions they made while listening.

EMPATHY

It's easier to work through any type of grievance when you develop the ability to respond empathetically. After all, demonstrating empathy doesn't mean you're agreeing with the client's point of view but that you're willing to acknowledge and respect it. It's the difference between saying, "I completely agree with everything you're saying" and "I completely understand everything you're saying." And it starts by vocalizing your desire to understand the other person's point of view. For instance, "I can see you're frustrated – help me understand what's going on so I can see things better from your perspective."

The more empathetic you are, the more you demonstrate to the client that you understand his or her reality. That gives them the confidence that you'll be able to work through future issues constructively.

For many in IT, I find this is an Achilles heel. Far too often, the IT professional's gut instinct is to defend him- or herself, cut off the other person or flat out make them wrong. "After all," they figure, "We've done our homework and know the right answer." But being an effective consultant isn't about the *right answer*. If others can't hear what you have to say because of how you deliver the message, you have lost your ability to influence. Delivery is everything. If I have an important point to make, the other person is much more likely to hear me if I have been equally interested in their perspective. How I demonstrate that respect is empathy. In most conversations, that can be a simple paraphrase or acknowledgment of their idea first, before I add my two cents.

DIPLOMACY

Closely related to empathy is diplomacy, which is being respectful to other people even when you don't agree with them. After all, you're not going to influence anyone with the attitude of, "I'm right, and you're an idiot." Or even, "You're wrong, and here's why."

When you find yourself disagreeing with a client – even when you're sure you're right – you have to keep it from becoming a battle of who's right and who's wrong. You need to take a step back and deliver your message in a way that the other person wants to listen to it.

Sometimes, it's even a matter of helping the other person save face – it's embarrassing and threatening for someone to realize they're wrong. So it's important to create a safe environment for the other person to become more knowledgeable and perhaps even change their opinion.

AVOIDING EMOTIONAL HOOKS

It's easy to get upset or angry when the people you're dealing with go on the attack or annoy you in other ways, like refusing to validate your competence or insisting their viewpoint is right. For many people, their first reaction is to push back, defend themselves, or throw up their hands and walk away. It's the fight-or-flight instinct. But once you're emotionally hooked, you are no longer objective, and your effectiveness as a consultant is diminished.

That's why another important skill to adopt for yourself and to teach your staff is developing the awareness to know what stirs your most passionate emotional responses. With this self-awareness, you can avoid taking other people's words personally, stay objective and see the situation for what it is.

At one client I've worked with, I was very intrigued by a development strategy one of the IT directors used with her staff. This is a world-renowned medical institution that literally deals with life-or-death issues. This director saw the value in helping her staff handle those "sticky" situations better. She knew that when tough situations are handled poorly, it can cause damage to key relationships. This director regularly stages "fire drills" at staff meetings based on real situations encountered in the past, to let the team practice managing their way through difficult emotional encounters. How would they react when a business unit vice president dresses them down and tells them they're a bunch of idiots who don't know what they're doing? By practicing their response, they'll have better options and more confidence when a similar event occurs in real life.

EDUCATING WITHOUT ARROGANCE

I've heard many IT departments complain that clients don't really know what they want, that they're unable to provide a clear set of requirements. But that would be akin to asking the client to provide a blueprint of a house when they've never built one before. It's up to the IT professional to educate business clients on what they don't know and do it in a way the client can understand. This is also a problem for those in IT who have other IT functional areas as clients. Even within IT, we don't always speak the same language. The same words can have very different meanings. In fact, I have found this to be an even bigger challenge with IT clients because we make many more assumptions when we think we understand.

First, you have to educate yourself on the language the client speaks and how to translate your knowledge in a way that works for them. And remember that just because IT professionals tend to be analytical and linear in their thinking, not everyone else is. And just because IT professionals tend to lay out the facts in a logical way, that doesn't mean the client will understand. You need to turn the tables around – what matters to them? What are their goals? What misperceptions do they have?

You also have to learn how to share your knowledge and expertise without being threatening, negative, arrogant or condescending. This often means being conscious of your word choices and tone of voice. Your goal is to help the client feel more confident, secure and engaged in the project.

For instance, what if the client is asking for changes that are outside the available time and budget constraints? They assume IT can "work its magic" and produce a system that does what they need. The temptation might be to tell them how unrealistic their request is. But what if you helped them become a better consumer of technology by educating them on what their request entails? Then, you could dig into what they're really asking for and agree to something that's close to what they want – something that's "good enough."

When you do this, you're also helping to market your organization, something we'll discuss in Chapter 9. Negative stereotypes aside, marketing is simply creating an awareness of your value by educating and communicating with clients.

RAPPORT BUILDING

Because of the time constraints facing IT departments today, many IT professionals consider it a goal to stick to the facts and minimize socializing during meetings and encounters with business clients. But what if they developed a closer relationship with the client? What kind of benefits would that provide?

Consider this scenario: You arrive in a client's cubicle for a scheduled one-on-one meeting, and she's excited about an email she just received with photographs from the previous weekend's celebration of her grandmother's 90th birthday party. She invites you to have a look before you start the meeting. How would you respond?

All too often, IT professionals might say, "We've got a lot to do today – can we continue with our agenda?" What a missed opportunity! This was the perfect chance to share a personal moment with the client and thus build some rapport.

I always recommend that you take your cues from the client. The bottom line is that people are much more willing to give others the benefit of the doubt if they feel a mutual connection. These encounters don't have to get touch-feely, but, for instance, if you see pictures of the client's child playing soccer on the desk, why not ask a few questions about it? It will only help you in the future, especially when a project gets rocky. With some individuals, you'll need to build rapport totally around the business because you may know very little about them personally.

Building rapport with individuals who are geographically dispersed requires more intentionality. I know many teams who send digital pictures to introduce themselves, and they make sure that if someone on the team is traveling to that location, they schedule a time to stop in and make personal contact. When working with global clients, rapport building often requires even more social contact and establishment of personal relationships.

SECTION 5
How Difficult Can This Be?

Like anything in life, the idea of developing consulting skills and learning to influence other people is simpler than the reality of doing so. For one thing, it requires IT and business clients to learn about each other's areas of expertise, and it takes time to do that. Amid the pressure today to "just do it," you may face some pushback. But in the end, it's more time-consuming to *not* approach things this way.

One business analyst I know was struck by an experience he had outside of work that really drove home this point. He and his wife wanted to add a fireplace to their home. They called three contractors, one of whom never called back and one who gave their bid over the phone. The third, however, asked if he could come to the analyst's house to meet him and his wife and see the room in which they wanted the fireplace. He drew up some sketches of different approaches, showing them what was possible, what it would involve and the cost for each idea. In the end, his bid was higher than the phone bid, but the analyst and his wife were hooked – they felt this contractor really understood what they wanted, and they looked forward to working with him, as they'd really developed a good rapport.

Did this take extra time? Sure it did, but the analyst and his wife were nearly guaranteed to be satisfied with the final outcome. Balancing the pressure to "just do it" and taking time to more clearly understand a client's needs will result in greater value. If you're not convinced, think of how your outside competition responds to your clients' requests for an IT solution – "Sure, we can do that!" – without really understanding the details.

Another reason you may get pushback is because of the IT organization's previous history with the client. Does the client have reason to trust that the organization would be a good partner, ready and able to operate as a valued consultant? If past experience has shown clients that working with IT takes too much time, money and effort, there's some reputation rebuilding to do.

This applies even if you just joined the company, and the bad experience with IT took place five years before. Clients can draw the conclusion after one debacle. They often paint all IT departments with the same brush. For better or worse, IT walks around with whatever baggage was created by previous experience, good bad or indifferent.

At one client I worked with, a business executive recounted to me when the CIO at the firm had announced a new organizational structure to better align the department with the business. "We laughed," the executive says. "We had not historically heard IT talk about the business at all – it was always about technology. So when they declared they wanted to be strategic business partners, we couldn't imagine it."

It took the CIO two years to establish the credibility the IT department needed to start partnering with the business. It involved building best practices, demonstrating an interest in understanding the business and talking with clients in their language.

It's not easy starting from behind the eight ball, but when you consider all the options, what better choice could you make? Our clients need a trusted partner to enable the business strategies that they're putting in place right now. Don't you want to be perceived as their partner of choice?

CONCLUSION

Business clients make decisions every day, big and small, and for those that involve technology, they need to work with someone they trust, a partner who can help them sort out what they really need from what they think they want. Like a good realtor, contractor, financial planner or doctor, IT professionals need to become that kind of partner – someone with both the technology expertise and the ability to apply it in ways that make them indispensable to the business.

And "indispensable" is exactly what IT organizations need to be. You need to put aside any pre-conceived notions of what a consultant does and realize that you need to become an internal consultant, yourself. Otherwise, there are plenty of external vendors and consultants who will happily do that job for you. But just like them, you can develop the skills and mindsets to influence your clients and – by doing so – they'll give you the opportunity to help make decisions that are best for both the business and the IT organization.

There's really no other choice for IT professionals today. You can either be the broker who lets her clients make the wrong investments for their needs – never to be called upon by those clients again – or you can develop the business acumen and human interaction skills that are the marks of a trusted partner.

Considerations for Evolving into the Role of Consultant

10. Stop making assumptions – paraphrase to check your understanding. Own the communications.

9. If you call a meeting, make it a good one.

8. If you're not bringing enthusiasm to work, you may be draining it from others (if you don't like what you're doing, it shows).

7. Ask good questions – uncover the issue instead of rushing in with a fix.

6. Learn diplomacy – be respectful even when you don't agree.

5. Deliver your message in way that others can hear it – avoid appearing arrogant and condescending.

4. Talk about what you can do, not what you can't – clients don't want to hear excuses; they want help solving their problem.

3. If trust breaks down, you need to address it head-on – ask your client what it will take to rebuild the relationship.

2. Educate clients to be better consumers of technology – you can play a huge role in increasing their confidence in your services.

1. When you take the position of being right, it implies someone else is wrong – or worse, an idiot. Instead, take time to listen so you can understand their perspective first.

SPECIFIC ACTIONS I WILL TAKE

✔

✔

✔

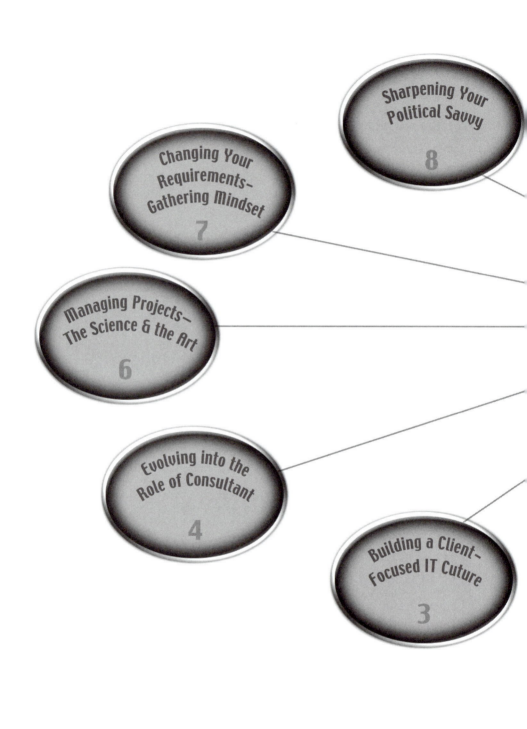

Sharpening Your
Political Savvy

8

Changing Your
Requirements-
Gathering Mindset

7

Managing Projects-
The Science & the Art

6

Evolving into the
Role of Consultant

4

Building a Client-
Focused IT Cuture

3

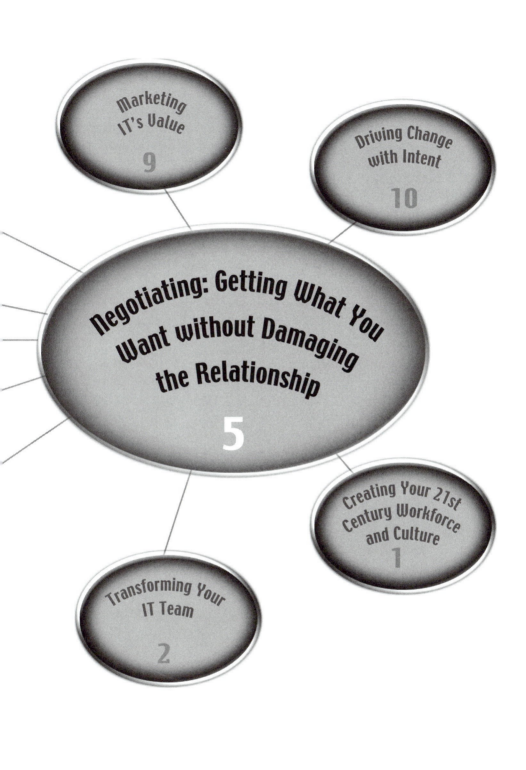

Marketing
IT's Value

9

Driving Change
with Intent

10

Negotiating: Getting What You
Want without Damaging
the Relationship

5

Creating Your 21st
Century Workforce
and Culture

1

Transforming Your
IT Team

2

not a day goes by that IT leaders and staff members don't negotiate with someone. My definition for negotiations is what happens when someone wants something from someone else, whether that person is a team member or a business client. Typically, each party states their case, and in one way or another, they come to an agreement, whether they're skilled or unskilled, and whether the process is emotional or neutral.

Think of a day in the life of the IT organization, where IT professionals at all levels face many types of negotiation situations every day, all day long. In order to launch a new application, they need to work with the business client to have them allocate some of their staff to test the application. Then they need to work with the IT server team to get the go-ahead to get some space on a server for testing. From there, they need to secure a slot on the applications staff's calendar to make sure the test system is loaded in time for the business group they just talked into doing the testing. Their success at securing these needed resources hinges on their ability to negotiate with clients and other IT staff.

Think about the help desk and various technical support staff, who need negotiation skills in order to ensure clients with critical needs don't get stuck in a queue waiting for IT support. And hardware techs often need to negotiate with software techs when coordinating upgrades for clients who simply can't wait six weeks for new application or technology capabilities. Clearly, the need for negotiation skills is as important to IT leaders as it is to their staffs. Money, people and time are all scarce in today's business world, and IT professionals are called upon to negotiate constantly for them.

However, the IT professionals I deal with usually lack the confidence for the negotiations that happen every day in their environment. Many like to believe that negotiating is what gets done on the vendor management team, and that it has nothing to do with leaders and staff personnel. And even if they are aware of how much they need to negotiate, many IT professionals are not at all sure how to do it and tend to avoid it. In fact, during my 27 years as a consultant and workshop leader at O&A, I've talked to IT professionals who are constantly under-staffed, don't have the right resources and need to meet unrealistic deadlines, all because of poor negotiation skills.

It doesn't have to be that way. It's my belief that to succeed in the IT profession today, all of IT – including leaders and the people who report to them – must get past their aversion to negotiating and learn how to manage the conflict that's an inevitable part of their everyday lives.

The good news is, good negotiators aren't born; they're taught. In fact, for a long time, I've strongly believed that IT could do a better job negotiating if they learned about something called "interest negotiations" rather than using "position negotiations," both of which I talk about later in this chapter. And on a personal note, while I was in the process of developing the negotiation workshop for O&A, my belief was strengthened even further when I went through the process of selling my home. My own negotiations cemented for me the difference between "interest negotiations" and "position negotiations," and as a result, I was able to get more out of the deal than I ever thought possible.

The most important thing about learning to be a skilled negotiator is changing your mindset about conflict and understanding that it's not something to avoid or downplay – it's a necessary component of two parties working out a difference of opinion. Conflict is an essential and inevitable part of life, so it's crucial to accept it and become aware of your own individual way of handling it. It is neither good nor bad; it's just a difference of opinion.

In the rest of this chapter, I'll provide an overview of other key mindset changes, as well as the negotiating skills and tools that I've learned about and found to be most effective in the IT world. Some of these concepts are informed by the highly influential negotiating reference books *Getting to Yes,* by Roger Fisher, William Ury and Bruce Patton (published by Random House Value Publishing, 1985), and *Bargaining for Advantage,* by G. Richard Shell (published by Penguin Books, 2006).

SECTION 1
"Position" vs. "Interest" Negotiations

Picture this scenario: Let's say your staff is working with the sales department on a project to set up a client-tracking system for the sales force. Your staff says it needs four people, two months and $25,000 to complete the project, while the sales department says it's willing to pay for two people, needs the system in three weeks and can budget only $10,000.

Can you feel the tension building? Does it seem inevitable that this conflict will quickly devolve into what some call "position negotiation," in which both IT and the client plant their stakes ever more firmly into the ground, each wondering why the heck the other can't understand their point of view? Certainly this is no way to start or maintain a good relationship with a client, let alone begin a project.

It doesn't have to be that way. In general, the customary practice in the U.S. is to try to resolve differences by negotiating based on "position" rather than on "interest." But it's not the only approach.

Look at a hypothetical scenario. Imagine two students, Jason and Sam, sitting across from one another at a table in a dorm room studying. Directly to their left is a window. Jason's position is that he wants the window closed, and Sam's position is that he wants it open. They begin negotiating by each taking a *position*. By taking positions, they find themselves at extremes – an open vs. closed window. The physical position of the window is the only item they are negotiating about because of the stakes they've put in the ground.

This negotiating style is inefficient and often ineffective. Positions limit negotiations because there's not a lot to negotiate over, and they create linear situations, with the participants starting at extreme endpoints and then moving along the continuum to some point where both agree to agree. In the case of Jason and Sam, the continuum is the physical window position – they can agree to have it completely open, completely closed or somewhere in between. It will take lot of time to come to an agreement because they started at extreme endpoints and will only make small concessions, which take time and energy. This also endangers the relationship because it becomes a contest of wills, and anger and resentment often results.

The alternative negotiating method is to negotiate based on our interests. Look at Jason's interests for wanting the window closed: There's a draft directly on his shoulder, and he's just getting over a cold and doesn't want to get sick again. He's only wearing a light short-sleeved shirt. The noise outside the window is distracting his studying.

Meanwhile, Sam might be pulling an all-nighter and wanting the cool air to help keep him awake. He doesn't have a cell phone and is waiting for his friend to yell up to him from the parking lot below to let him know he's arrived.

By talking about interests, the scope of potential negotiating possibilities increases dramatically. The two of them now can generate a list of options based on the different interests they have just stated. Jason might negotiate about changing seats with Sam so the draft isn't on his shoulders. Sam might get some coffee or high-caffeine drink to keep him awake. Jason might suggest that Sam have his friend call him on

Jason's cell phone when he arrives. They might agree to open a totally different window that would give Sam some air but not directly impact Jason. They are now discussing multiple options that have nothing to do with the physical position of the window – in fact, the window doesn't even come up in the discussion, whereas it was the only thing they were discussing before.

That's because interests define each party's real needs, wants or concerns. They are broader than and can be very different from stated positions. When you understand your own interests as well as those of the other party, you can spend your time developing possible options, not fighting over small concessions about one item.

Let's go back to the sales example introduced earlier. The typical negotiating method would be for the IT department to start from its end of the three positions (number of people, time and budget), while the sales department starts from the other end of the same three positions. The two sides would move linearly toward each other, hopefully coming to a common ground both can agree on. This is *position* negotiating. The options are limited, which makes the negotiation results very limited.

But what if the IT department's *interests* include the fact that the department is about to hire two new people who will start in three weeks. This small sales project would be a perfect way of getting the new hires familiar with their new environment, rather than starting them immediately on a complex project. The sales department has two people going on extended leave and wants them trained before they go, so that when they return, the ramp-up time is quicker.

Now IT and sales can broaden their negotiating stand. IT might stick with its timeframe of two months but offer to do the project with five people instead of four, while lowering the budget from $25,000 to $10,000. IT might even suggest to sales that if it expands the budget to $25,000 and is willing to wait two months, it will add a whole bunch of desirable bells and whistles to the program. At this point, IT has moved away from the linearity of position negotiating (two vs. four people, three weeks vs. two months, $10,000 vs. $25,000) to something much broader, such as training new hires (which is an interest of IT) and expanding the scope of the project (which is an interest of sales). They can also offer to train the sales force on a prototype before they leave, therefore helping speed up their use of the new system later.

SECTION 2:

Three Key Factors; Three-Step Process

When we think about negotiating, we often picture two parties sitting across from each other at the bargaining table. But in actuality, there are three steps to the negotiating process: planning/preparation, the information exchange and, finally, bargaining. In each of these steps, we need to address three key factors: negotiating elements; people and relationships; and styles and situations.

I like to depict the three-step process as a stairway, and the three key factors as a railing (see below). The railing supports each step of the stairway, and you have to ascend the stairway one step at a time, without skipping any step.

In my workshop, I start by discussing the railing – or the three key factors – as they look in the first step: preparation and planning. Anyone who's ever painted a room in their house has discovered – either the easy way or the hard way – that planning and preparation are as important as and can take longer than the actual painting. The same can be said of negotiating, and yet many people involved with negotiations fail to expend the effort on this stage that they should.

Standing on this first step, we begin to establish the first key factor on the railing – our negotiation elements.

NEGOTIATION ELEMENTS

Positions, Interests and Options. The first element involves assessing your positions, interests and options, as well as those of the other party. This means analyzing what's important to you and your clients, in terms of positions, interests and options. So whereas your position is something you've decided on ("we can finish that project in three months"), your interests are what caused you to make that decision ("we've got five other projects going on," "we just lost a key database analyst," etc.). Everyone in virtually every situation has multiple interests, and these need to be brought to the table so that you aren't limited by positions.

That's why you want to list *all* your interests before you sit down at the negotiating table. The typical items IT negotiates for are money, time (due date), people (resources), scope, standards, policies and procedures. If you understand your own interests, you're in a much better position to be creative about the options you propose and how you respond to those that are proposed to you.

Let's take another look at Jason and Sam. If Sam understood his need to stay awake as an interest, he could have concentrated on other options that would keep him awake besides the physical position of the window. You're in a much better position if you can stay flexible, and that means being prepared to offer and accept a range of options.

But it's not a one-way street – it's also important to understand the needs and concerns of your clients so you can anticipate what their reactions are likely to be and what leverage they might have over you. Do some background work to determine the other party's interests and options.

Criteria, Leverage, Bottom Line and "BATNA." You also need to establish some criteria that you and the other party can use as a fair measurement of whether you've reached an equitable agreement. For instance, are there some industry best practices you can use to establish the amount of time you need to complete the project? Or maybe, if you've had a successful project with this client in the past, you can suggest using the same benchmarks as the criteria for starting negotiations on this project. For example, if you dedicated two days a week to the past project and it was successful, you can suggest doing the same on this project.

You also need to think about leverage. Leverage is created from the balance of fears and needs, based on which side has more to lose from a failure to agree. So, the more a party has to lose, the less leverage it has, and the less it has to lose, the more leverage it has.

Two additional pieces of information that need to be considered are your bottom line and your BATNA (or best alternative to a negotiated agreement). Your bottom line defines what you absolutely can't "give" on. Meanwhile, BATNA is a concept developed by negotiation researchers Roger Fisher, William Ury and Bruce Patton. It refers to the courses of action that are at your disposal if the current negotiations fail – in other words, your Plan B.

Knowing your BATNA helps you know when to walk away from the negotiations. For instance, if you know you can resell something – say a car – to a used dealer for $10,000, the bottom line helps you be better equipped to resist making a bad decision, such as selling it for $7,000 in the pressure of the moment. To determine your BATNA, you would also take into consideration the steps you would have to take if the negotiations were to fail. For instance, you would have to find a buyer other than the used dealer, and you'd have to pay to advertise the car, research the required paperwork and possibly even postpone your new car purchase. Knowing what your alternative steps are if you walk away from the negotiations helps you be more flexible than just having a bottom line because you can readily compare your alternative plan to what's on the table. It may sometimes be worth putting aside your "set" bottom line because the alterative options if you walk away are not as good as what is currently on the table. When you reach the point that your alternatives (BATNA) are better than what you are being offered in the negotiations, this tells you to walk away.

PEOPLE AND RELATIONSHIPS

Further along the railing but still on the first step, we address the second key factor: people and relationships. During this phase, you need to assess the degree of trust you have with the people you're negotiating with and work to repair any poor or nonexistent relationships.

It's easy to overlook the importance of relationships during negotiations and focus only on substance. In my work with IT clients, I find most are more comfortable discussing "things" than "feelings." But avoiding relationship issues is only an option if you have no intention of ever dealing with the people you're negotiating with again. Most often, that's not the case for IT professionals, who deal mainly with internal clients. Once a project ends, you're bound to work with these same people again, down the road.

For this reason, it's really important not to blow the relationship, and ideally, you should strive to strengthen the relationship so that the next project gets off to an even better start. When a relationship is good, it creates trust and confidence, which can help smooth over the rough spots in future negotiations. Without it, even relatively easy negotiations can be difficult. We discuss the relationship-building process more fully in Chapter 4 on consulting skills.

STYLES AND SITUATIONS

The last key factor on the railing is "styles and situations." During the planning/preparation step, you need to determine your own negotiating style, as well as that of the other party. Most people actually have two or three preferred styles, based on the way they prefer to handle conflict. Using *Bargaining for Advantage* and the Thomas-Kilmann Conflict Mode Instrument, I define five different styles, ranging from passive to aggressive.

- **Competitors:** Like to win and control negotiations by using demands, threats and ultimatums.

- **Problem solvers:** Encourage each party to talk about their interests and then find a solution by brainstorming many options. This style works well in complex negotiations, but it's not so practical when time is short or the other party isn't willing to work with you.

- **Compromisers:** Look for quick, obvious and fair solutions to bargaining problems, like splitting the difference.

- **Accommodators:** Tend to resolve interpersonal conflicts by solving the other person's problem.

- **Avoiders:** Strongly dislike interpersonal conflict and try to avoid situations that might cause conflict. They try very hard to arrange their personal and professional lives so that conflict is at a minimum.

You also have to take your best guess at the style of the person you're negotiating with. Don't assume the other party approaches conflict the same way you do, or you could get your lunch eaten. Imagine an "accommodator" assuming that a "competitor" also wants to help solve the opposing party's problems!

In addition to assessing your client's negotiation style, you also have to think about the bargaining situation you're entering into. There are four basic situations, and each one is based on two characteristics: the importance of the substance you're negotiating on and the importance of the future relationship you have with the opposing party.

The graphic below – based on *Bargaining for Advantage* – illustrates the four situations. In the top two quadrants, the importance of the future relationship with the opposing party is high. These are the most common bargaining situations for IT professionals, who almost always negotiate with people they'll need to work with again in the future.

In the top left quadrant, the substance of the negotiations is less important than the relationship you're trying to build, maintain or mend. For instance, you might be willing to throw in more bells and whistles or charge less if you're just getting to know a new client or are trying to repair a poor relationship. The emphasis is on the relationship, not the substance being negotiated.

The upper right quadrant represents the situation I feel IT professionals find themselves in most of the time. The relationship is very important, but with limited budgets and resources, you can't just give away the farm, so the substance of the conflict is also important. That's why I call it the "balancing act." In this situation, you have to be prepared not to back down in negotiations and make promises on substance issues that you can't keep – i.e., dates, scope, priorities. Otherwise, despite your best efforts, the client will see only missed deadlines and failed delivery. At the same time, focusing only on substance and ignoring the relationship can destroy the project just as quickly.

The bottom two quadrants happen less often. The lower left quadrant is a situation where the relationship and the substance of negotiations are equally low in importance. It might be a quick favor for one person who needs to accomplish something that's not particularly strategic to the company, like a simple report. It's not a big deal, it takes little time, and it has no impact on future dealings.

A one-time deal, on the other hand, is when the substance is more important than the relationship. It's easy to make the mistake of thinking you're

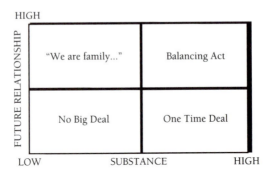

in this type of bargaining situation when you're really not. For instance, a client may ask you to install a new release or code some extra features. You see this as just more work, i.e., as a substance issue. Many IT professionals will only want to negotiate on substance and tell the client, "No, it's outside of scope." That's when it's time to do some homework to assess how important the request is to the client's business and whether you can take the opportunity to strengthen the relationship with this client by accommodating the "substance" request.

SECTION 3

Applying the Key Factors to the Second Step: Information Exchange

Now we move up to step two, the information exchange. In this phase, you meet face-to-face with the opposing party, but you're not in the bargaining phase yet. Whereas the first step was all about doing lots of preliminary legwork and researching the three key factors, the second step is when you can really see if your assessments are correct, and can clear up and get information you don't have. It's time for both parties to get their perceptions out in the open, and state their interests and issues.

Through conversation and observation, you determine during the information exchange things such as whether you were right about the client's interests and opinions, whether they trust IT as much as you thought they did, whether you guessed correctly at their bargaining style and if you're in the bargaining situation you thought you were in. It's when you can really see whether you were right about your assessments during the planning and preparation step.

For instance, I might sit down with the client, thinking I'm coming into a "balancing act" situation (upper right quadrant), where both the substance of the negotiations and the relationship have equal importance. But I'm unaware that before I joined the company, they'd worked on a major project with IT that ended in disaster. During the information exchange, I ask them if this is their first major project with the IT organization, and they answer with an emotional description of the former debacle.

Finding this out, I need to correct my assessment and readjust for a "We are Family" bargaining situation (upper left quadrant), since I've determined the relationship is shaky and needs to be strengthened.

Here's another example: I've never met the particular client before, but I researched what he was like by talking with others who'd worked with him. Through that legwork, I determined that he typically uses a compromiser style in negotiations. During the information exchange, I look around his office and ask him about his golf trophies. He responds by telling me he loves golf but hates team sports because he doesn't like to depend on other people to help him win. With that comment, I realize he's more of a competitor than a compromiser and plan to adjust my bargaining style accordingly.

Notice that this second step is all about dialogue, relationship building and establishing rapport. Put simply, no one is going to tell you anything until they trust you. If you want to hear the other person's interests and point of view, you need to build a rapport. So if you have a poor relationship with the client, make sure you mend it before moving to the bargaining step. We discuss building rapport and relationships in more detail in Chapter 4 on consulting skills.

It's also important during this second step to actively listen to what the client has to say. Active listening means you ask questions when you don't understand what is being said and paraphrase your understanding of what the client is saying. This isn't the time to argue or shut down the dialog. The most important thing during the information exchange stage is to keep the dialogue flowing, even if you find yourself vehemently disagreeing with the other party. Once the dialogue ends, the negotiations are over. In my workshops, I teach a method called "disagreeing diplomatically," which focuses on keeping a discussion going when you want to say no.

SECTION 4

The Final Step: Now Comes the Bargaining

Finally, we move to the top and final step: Bargaining. In this step, you use all the information you've gathered and vetted in the first and second steps. You know your own interests and options, as well as the opposing party's. You've established criteria and your bottom line. You're sure of the bargaining situation you're getting into, the negotiation style you're going to use and the style you're going to encounter. Now you're ready to bargain.

Bargaining is mainly made up of exchanges, concessions and deal-making. It's where you determine who will give and get what. It's also where you will likely encounter tactics that are used differently by people depending on their different negotiating styles.

What's important to realize is that people with different negotiation styles have different views of what's fair and ethical. The tactics you decide to use are very much intertwined with the kind of person you are – you can't separate the way you act in negotiations from the person you are in life. The best advice is to let your conscience be your guide.

Meanwhile, it's very important to recognize when tactics are being used negatively against you and what your possible counter moves should be. Knowing how to respond beforehand will keep you from reacting emotionally. Here are five of the most common bargaining tactics I've seen people use over my years in the IT profession:

The hot potato: They get you to take on their problem by making it your problem. A good countermove is to refuse to take ownership and instead generate options they can take.

Appeal to a higher authority: They postpone a decision to take it to someone of greater authority. A good countermove is to find out what they *are* able to commit to before you begin bargaining.

The flinch: They try to get concessions by having you react to their overstated emotion, usually a dramatic verbal or nonverbal negative response to a proposal. A good countermove is to not react emotionally and show confusion as a reaction to their outburst.

Nibbling: The goal of this is to try to get a little bit more once the other party thinks the negotiations are over. The extra issue or demand is so "small," it doesn't sound worth spoiling the deal after so much investment. A good countermove is to offer to open up negotiations all over again to include this new item.

Reciprocity ploys: They make small concessions while asking you for big ones. A good countermove is to take a break when you feel pressured and consider the overall situation before making your next move.

CONCLUSION: EFFECTIVE NEGOTIATORS ARE MADE, NOT BORN

Many IT professionals might feel new to the negotiations scene, or they might think negotiations don't include them, but that's not true. Negotiations are something people in IT engage in every day, with peers, subordinates, bosses and clients. And the only way to feel more comfortable and confident in this role is to learn about the techniques that experienced negotiators employ and practice them consistently.

A good place to begin is realizing that negotiating doesn't start at the bargaining table. It takes time to plan and prepare your side – both your position and your interests – and find out the same about your client. The more options and interests you bring to the table and the more flexibility you have, the better deal you can make.

I hear IT professionals claim they just don't have the time to engage in this three-step process. What they need to realize is it's more than time spent; it's an investment made – an investment that will serve them in developing and maintaining better relationships, more reasonable deadlines, adequate resources and positive outcomes. Resources are scarce in today's business world, and we're called upon to negotiate constantly for them, in the form of money, people and time. If you want to get the resources you need, and the relationships that help you get them, you've got to become a skilled negotiator and teach your staff to do the same.

Remember that no one is asking you to be something you're not. There are all sorts of negotiating styles; it's up to you to determine which one is right for you. At the end of the day, you still need to have a relationship with the other party after the negotiations end. It's a fine balance between getting what you and the other party needs and maintaining a healthy business relationship with our clients.

Getting your head in the negotiating game doesn't have to be stressful. It's all about confronting your anxieties, changing your mindset, being yourself and – perhaps most important of all – knowing how to prepare.

Approaches for Getting What You Want without Damaging the Relationship

10. Remember Ben Franklin's words: "If you fail to prepare, you prepare to fail."

9. The single-answer approach inhibits creating options. Be flexible and open to various options.

8. Relationships and rapport count.

7. Know your preferred negotiation styles.

6. Be clear on which of the four bargaining situations you are negotiating within.

5. The cheapest concession to give the other party is to listen to them.

4. Don't close the negotiation door by saying "no;" disagree diplomatically.

3. Be prepared to recognize tactics during bargaining and effectively counter them.

2. Be aware that you negotiate every day, within your IT team and with clients, and learn from each experience.

1. The benefits of effective negotiations: You improve the chances you will get what you need and want, and you'll keep your client relationship solid.

SPECIFIC ACTIONS I WILL TAKE

✔

✔

✔

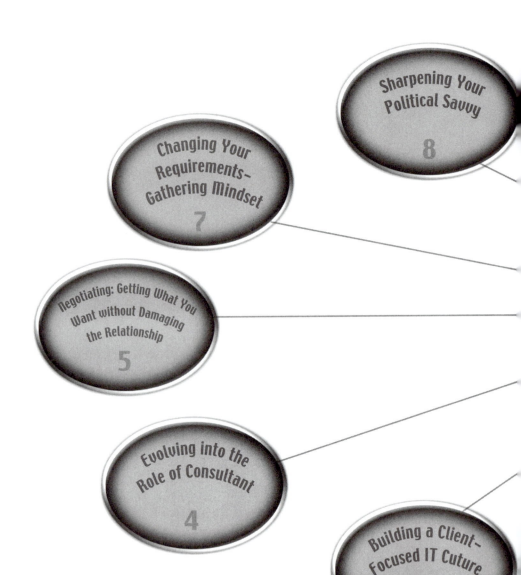

Sharpening Your
Political Savvy

8

Changing Your
Requirements-
Gathering Mindset

7

Negotiating: Getting What You
Want without Damaging
the Relationship

5

Evolving into the
Role of Consultant

4

Building a Client-
Focused IT Cuture

3

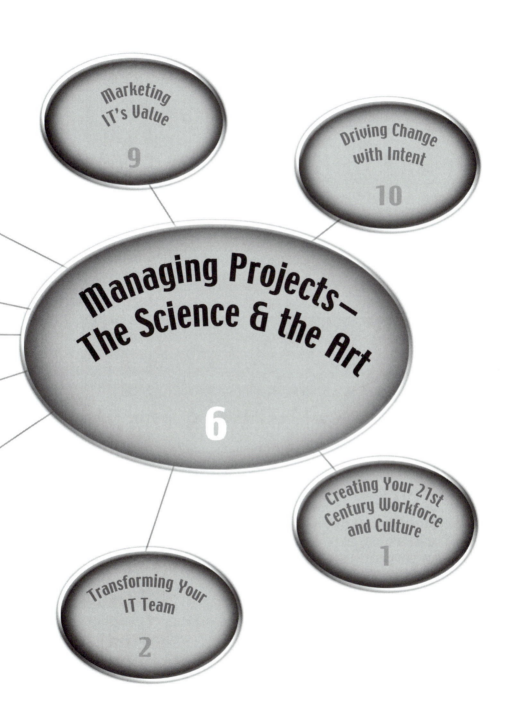

Marketing
IT's Value

9

Driving Change
with Intent

10

Managing Projects—
The Science & the Art

6

Creating Your 21st
Century Workforce
and Culture

1

Transforming Your
IT Team

2

It's a generally agreed-upon statistic that about 25% of technology projects are deemed successful. If the engineering field had the same number of project failures, no one would ever ride in an elevator or fly in an airplane! Whether you concur with this abysmal statistic or not, I think we can all agree that it's time we boost our project success rate.

The fact is, IT project management is a relatively young discipline, especially when compared with other industries. In construction, engineering and defense contracting, project management is significantly better understood, supported and practiced, and project managers and their clients in these fields generally benefit from a higher level of professional maturity. They can rely on documented historical records of prior project undertakings, more formal authority granted to the project manager, enhanced regulatory and QA oversight, greater emphasis on formal educational qualifications, mandatory licensing and certification requirements, genuine legal liability for malfeasance or poor quality and a more responsible understanding of the role of project sponsor. Does any of this sound even vaguely familiar within the world of IT?

In 1981, the Project Management Institute (PMI) set out a goal to establish project management as a unique discipline and an independent profession. It has been incredibly successful in meeting that goal. Project management is the predominant management style of the 21st century, complete with professional certification and a growing body of knowledge.

Yet for all the acknowledgement of the importance of project management to modern companies, the role of the IT project manager is often tenuous at best. During my 20 years as an independent consultant, I have witnessed too many instances of what can be described only as project management malpractice. Even the selection and development of project managers is so often dictated by convenience or corporate inertia that it can be regarded as the accidental profession.

On one hand, IT projects have benefited from the advent of dedicated project management offices, more powerful planning tools and the growing importance of project management certification. On the other, IT projects continue to be plagued with problems that are decades old.

At the beginning of every project management workshop I've taught, I've conducted an informal survey of the kinds of problems faced by the organization's IT projects. Over the years, the results have shown a troubling set of nagging problems. You could even call them systematic in nature. Participants constantly list project management challenges such as:

unreasonable and/or predefined due dates, lack of executive management support, inadequate resources, ill-defined or changing requirements, poor or shifting priorities, politics and insufficient client participation.

The really sad part of the exercise is the litany of problems listed from the client's perspective. With stunning regularity, participants list problems like too much red tape and bureaucracy, IT-imposed solutions, missed deadlines, blown budgets, not being kept properly informed and a failure to provide business benefit and value. Too often, IT projects epitomize Yogi Berra's wry observation, "This is like déjà vu all over again."

That's why it's so important for IT leaders to recognize that project management is not just a scientific endeavor comprising knowledge of tools and methodologies. There's an art to managing projects that requires a mindset I just don't see very often in companies across the country today.

Perhaps the best way to describe that mindset is to tell you about my background. I began my IT career 33 years ago as an EDP auditor in a bank. I was assigned to oversee the conduct and results of internal IT projects. In addition to making sure that the system being developed was well controlled, I was also charged with assessing if the process for building the system was well controlled. During my four years as an auditor, I witnessed project management behavior that varied from the truly accomplished and sublime to the kind of foolishness that bordered on professional incompetence.

I then transferred into a systems development department and quickly learned that the job of an IT project manager was challenging on the best of days. One fact became very clear: A project manager has a lot more responsibility than formal authority.

Fortunately, I had the opportunity to work with some outstanding project managers who impressed me with not only their technical capability but also their professional "charm." In the absence of authority, these project managers got things done by influencing their clients, team members and project stakeholders. In other words, they relied on their ability to forge meaningful relationships and to act in an influential way. The concept of "influence" is so important, we've covered it in depth in Chapter 4, on consulting skills.

What I learned is that while techniques, tools, and technology are important, it's relationship-building and interpersonal skills that are essential to project management success. Years later, I still refer to the project management workshop I developed as "a three-day charm school for project managers."

Today, good IT leaders realize that successful project managers are those trained to master the human side of their projects, as much as the supporting tools and methodologies. They have learned that projects succeed for one reason and one reason only: because the people on the project succeed. That's right; even if the project team misses a target date or blows the budget, a project can still be successful if the client perceives that the team was responsive and competent and achieved the objectives of the project.

So much of what we do in IT is project-based. That's why, so far in this book, we've concentrated on mindsets and skills that indirectly contribute to enhanced project delivery. In this chapter, I'll dive into the heart of project management itself, focusing on how IT leaders can improve their organization's project success rate by changing their mindsets and improving how they structure, plan and manage projects. Then, in the following two chapters, we'll continue on the project management theme by showing IT leaders how they can change their organization's approach to gathering business requirements (Chapter 7) and navigate corporate politics (Chapter 8).

SECTION 1
The Building Blocks of Project Management

Let's start by looking more closely at the term, "project management." It really doesn't fairly describe the job at all, because in actuality, the "management" part of the job is the final phase of a three-phase process. In my project management workshop, I've distilled the job of a project manager down into a group of essential processes, and arranged them in to three phases: structuring, planning and managing.

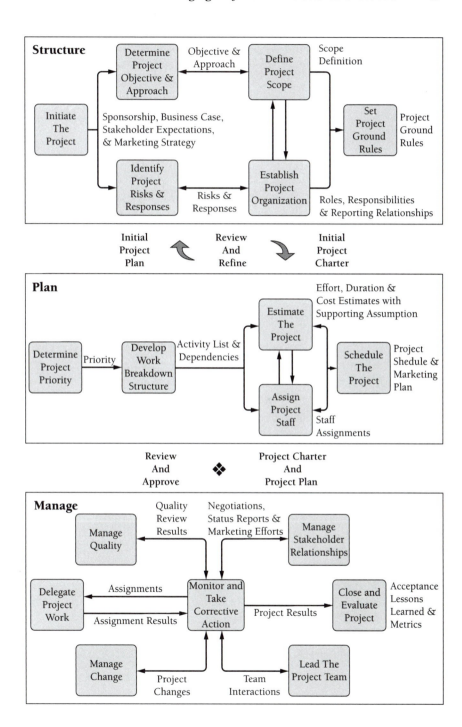

The first two phases – structuring and planning – should consume more of a project manager's time than the last phase. And none of the stages can be approached mechanically. From what I've seen, most project managers also need to undergo a mindset shift to focus on the real goal of any project: client satisfaction.

Imagine a homeowner having a pool built in his backyard. He hasn't done a lot of research into what size pool his lot will accommodate, how the excavator will get in, whether any water, sewer, electric or cable lines will have to be re-routed, whether he wants a plaster or quartz interior, etc. He's not thinking about his current landscaping being decimated during the digging process, the weather holdups, the debris scattered about his backyard while he waits for yet another sub-contractor who fails to show up. He's just picturing himself and his family cannonballing into the refreshing water on a 90-degree day.

In order for this project to end in "success," the pool company representative has a lot of upfront work to do, starting with structuring the project. His first task is to gain an appreciation for who in the family is the sponsor and who is the client. In our workshops, we prefer the term "client" to "sponsor," if for no other reason than "sponsor" sounds so fiduciary in nature. We also believe that the concept of "client" orients the project to more of a service relationship vs. a simple business transaction. And as any happy couple can attest, there can be a world of difference between dealing with the person who writes the checks and working with the person who has to be happy with the color of the tile.

Next, the pool rep has to work with this family of stakeholders on thinking about how they intend to use the pool – do they intend to swim laps, install a diving board or float around drinking blender drinks? That might be called the project "objective." Are they imagining an outdoor shower, lights, solar heater, spa and a pool house? That's the project "scope." Is there time in the schedule and money in the budget to do all of this? Will the homeowners' association approve the design? These are the "project constraints." Do they understand what might happen when excavation begins (also known as "defining risk"), the type of communication they should expect and when final payment is due (which is called "setting ground rules")?

Only after completing this phase should the pool rep begin planning the project. This means breaking down the project into smaller parts and determining the order in which each piece should be accomplished (called the "work breakdown structure"), providing the homeowner with cost and time estimates, deciding which subcontractors to work with (also known as "assigning project staff") and publishing a schedule that's accessible to everyone.

Finally, it's time to break ground. This involves making sure the excavation crew, concrete workers, plumber, electrician and other workers understand what they're supposed to do (also called "work delegation") and checking on their work to be sure it's up to snuff (known as "quality reviews"). But what if the excavators hit water? What if the pool's planned location doesn't leave enough room for the excavation equipment? What if equipment breaks down? What if the decking color doesn't come out right? For any of these glitches, the pool rep will need to negotiate schedule, budget and design changes with the workers and the homeowner (called "change management" and "managing stakeholder relationships"). When the pool and landscaping are finally complete to the owner's satisfaction, it's time to close out the project, including a review of lessons learned and metrics that can be carried over into the next project.

Now imagine what would happen if the pool rep didn't do any of the upfront structuring and planning activities. The first obstacle to come along would likely result in one angry homeowner, thus setting up a rocky road for the entire duration of the project. In the end, the pool may get built, but at what cost? The only way the homeowner will deem the project a "success" is if he perceives the overall experience as mostly positive, and that depends in large part on the upfront time spent on defining, structuring and planning.

And it's not just the structuring, planning and management activities themselves that are important. During all this time that he's engaging with the homeowners, the pool rep is using a tool that IT people don't think about very much – his own personality and his ability to establish a relationship and even a rapport with the homeowners. Let's face it; things go wrong with any complex undertaking, and working through those obstacles is a lot easier when you have a strong partnership with the client.

And that's the real job of the project manager: developing a partnership with the project sponsor and key clients, involving them in structuring and planning the project and then using well-honed project management techniques to see it through to completion.

Section 2
Structuring Projects for Success

Now we'll take a closer look at the individual building blocks of project management. We'll start with structuring.

The first job of a project manager is to take an assignment and turn it into a project. However, merely defining a project is not enough. Projects must be structured for success. The most crucial work in this project initiation phase is sponsor/client identification. Many of the problems associated with IT projects can be traced back to poor or non-existent sponsorship. If the sponsor and client are not the same person, then it's vital that the project manager understand the role of each on the project.

For example, who provides the strategic direction for the project? Who is funding it? Who will benefit from it? Who will provide resources for it? Who will approve deliverables? Who can approve changes to the project? Who needs to know project status?

In the end, project initiation is the ultimate "moment of truth" for project managers. This first contact with the client sets the tone for the remainder of the project. It requires the utmost in tact and charm.

After initiation, the project manager continues project structuring by framing the project's business case and specifying business benefits, understanding project constraints, developing a solution strategy for the project and determining its objective. It's important to mention that the project manager needs to have sufficient domain knowledge in order to ask the right questions whose answers will frame the business case.

Once the objective is confirmed by the client, the project manager can set project scope. Project scope is defined as the suite of deliverables produced over the life of the project to prove that the objective was met. Simply put, the scope statement is a comprehensive list of what results are "in" and "out" of the project. As a quality assurance step, the project manager validates that the scope statement's list of deliverables is complete and sufficient to meet the project's objective.

Next, the project manager identifies project risks and possible mitigation strategies, and he establishes the project's organizational structure (roles, responsibilities and reporting relationships). The final process in structuring is establishing the all-important ground rules for conducting the project. The results of project structuring are documented in the project charter.

SECTION 3
Developing Plans That Work

The second phase in our three-phase approach is planning the project. While the perspective of structuring is "big picture" and strategic in nature, planning is detail-oriented and tactical. For instance, the essence of structuring is figuring out who are the key players on the project, what do they want and why is it important to them. On the other hand, planning focuses on how and when it will be accomplished, as well as by whom.

Project planning begins with an understanding of the relative priority of the newly defined project work to everything else on the project manager's plate. Prioritization is the interplay between the urgency of the work (i.e., due date) and the value or importance of the work. Enterprises without good work prioritization processes often tend to spend their scarce and expensive IT staff on urgent work rather than important work. One of the hallmarks of an effective IT organization is its ability to focus talent on high-value work with laser-like precision.

Once a project manager has received clear marching orders, he or she can begin planning the project in earnest. The heart of project planning is developing a good understanding of the work to de done. The process is called developing a "work breakdown structure," or WBS. A WBS is a purpose-built list of tasks to be accomplished on the project. The key to a good WBS is linking every task to a deliverable in the project charter's scope statement. Smart project managers will endeavor to involve team members in developing the WBS because this gives the people who will do the work some say in what work needs to be done. A well-defined WBS will make the next planning process – estimating the work – much easier.

An estimate is often referred to as an educated guess. The hard part is getting sufficiently educated about the project before the guessing begins. At O&A, our systematic approach to structuring and planning is intended to educate the people involved in estimating well enough to do a credible job.

There are many ways to estimate a project, including SWAGs, bottom-up, resident expert, analogous and parametric. There is also an array of automated tools for estimating IT projects. Unfortunately, while most IT shops have planning/scheduling tools, many do not own or use estimating tools. In the absence of using estimating tools, my experience has shown Delphi or consensus-based estimating to work very well. A Delphi estimate draws on the collective experience of multiple estimators to develop a reasonable range estimate with supporting assumptions. Performed with knowledgeable participants in a consensus manner, a Delphi estimate is second only to estimating tools in its accuracy.

Staffing the project can occur in tandem with estimating. In fact it's a good practice to involve team members who will be doing the work in estimating the work. What I like to emphasize here is that the project manager needs to be involved in helping to select the team. Unfortunately, that's not often what happens; in fact, one of the most common complaints about staffing that I hear in my workshops is the project manager's lack of say over who will participate on the project. All too often, the only criterion for team membership is availability, and the critical process of staffing a project team ends up being a poor take on musical chairs. The haphazard formation of project teams speaks volumes about the perceived importance and value of teamwork within an organization.

The final process in developing a project work plan is scheduling the work. Once again, the importance of this effort is lost because of how it is often performed. A lot of project schedules are simply manufactured out of thin air. A specified due date is given, and the project manager endeavors to fit the project into the available time between the "when" and "now." The insidious nature of this form of reverse engineering turns the entire process of planning into a cruel joke. With so much "winking and nodding" going on, it's a miracle that whiplash is not a more common occurrence on IT projects.

Overall, though, we have to remember that the project plan is separate from the reality of doing the project. A good plan should lay out a reasonable and feasible approach to the project. However, it is a guide and, as such, will be subject to revision based on the reality of the work. Years ago, I had the pleasure of belonging to a Civil Air Patrol search and rescue organization. As part of briefing search pilots, we would constantly remind them that the map is not the terrain. The same holds true for projects – the plan is the map, not the terrain.

Regrettably, I have witnessed good project managers turning themselves into human pretzels trying to get reality to fit the plan. Such is not the way of the world.

SECTION 4
Managing to Successful Completion

The final phase of our three-phase approach is managing the project. As can be seen from Sections 2 and 3 above, O&A's approach places a lot of emphasis on preparation before execution. Now, with preparations completed, the "real work" can now begin, as many of my workshop participants are eager to point out. I always find it striking how telling that comment is about a company's IT project culture.

Managing the actual work of a project involves seven sub-processes. The first three are inter-related and interactive processes that form the core of what I refer to as the essential "mechanics" of managing the work.

1. PROJECT DELEGATION

The first overt act of managing a project is delegation, or the process of getting the work off the plan and into the hands of the project team members. On the surface, delegation appears to be a mundane process, and it's true that during my career I've met many people who consider it a very pedestrian skill. However, most of these same people will also readily admit that they've been on the receiving end of poor delegation situations.

In my workshops, we conduct an exercise to identify some of the reasons why project managers don't delegate very well. The reasons most often cited include ego, fear of conflict, fear of failure, (the petty) fear of success, "I can do it faster or better," ignorance, lack of authority, control problems and trust issues. What's very illuminating about this exercise is that most participants recognize that the reasons they list are nothing more than excuses for not doing an important part of the project management job.

Time pressures often exaggerate the problem. What should be a thoughtful and collaborative process is all too often truncated into a perverse form of "dumping" on a team member. Regrettably, this can damage the relationship between the project manager and the team member.

2. MANAGING QUALITY

The second inter-related process is managing quality. If a project manager is not actively ensuring the management of a high-quality product, then what is he or she really managing? The approach I like to advocate is based on a traditional blend of defect prevention and defect detection.

For instance, I'm a strong believer in the benefits of conducting quality reviews, which is a visual inspection of any project deliverable, with the purpose of finding mistakes in that deliverable. People are generally very good at finding mistakes in other people's work, and smart project managers will capitalize on this very human tendency.

In addition, there's a very important serendipitous aspect associated with the defect-detection job of doing reviews: A well-performed quality review, timed appropriately in the development lifecycle, is also a very good defect prevention technique. A well-managed review process is the basis of all quality management and the essential precursor to all testing efforts. Results of the quality-review process provide the project manager with critical insight and input into the management function.

3. Managing Change

The third inter-related process is managing change. It's a simple fact of life that change happens, especially on large IT-based projects. Change is inevitable and must be properly dealt with. The current crop of "agile methodologies" pride themselves on their advocacy of embracing change during systems development. This is not only a sound development practice; it's also a good management practice.

The focus of change management is to provide the client with a realistic assessment of the impacts associated with a requested change. Once clients understand the impacts, they can make an informed business decision regarding the acceptance, deferral or rejection of the change. A good change management process will also provide the project manager with valuable insight into the dynamics of the project. The practice of leading change is so important that we've dedicated an entire chapter to it (see Chapter 10).

4. Monitoring and Taking Corrective Action

The focal points of the three processes we've discussed so far are monitoring and taking corrective action. Monitoring – which involves the collection, analysis and presentation of project performance data – is "passive," from the standpoint that it only provides the project manager with an understanding of project status. Taking corrective action – which requires the project manager to do something about the situation – is the "active" portion of the equation.

During my tenure as an IT manager, the one quality I cherished the most in a project manager was a bias for action. My constant admonishment was, "Lead, follow or get out of the way, but for the sake of the project, do something." I always preferred guiding a project manager vs. having to build a fire under one. A perennial trick question in project management is, "How does a project get a year behind?" The answer, of course, is one day at a time. Therefore, the project must be actively managed every single day. There is no autopilot.

5. Managing Stakeholder Relationships

The next two processes are often regarded as the "soft" side of project management, but actually, experience has shown them to be the real "hard" work on a project. Managing stakeholder relationships is the underlying philosophy of O&A's overall approach to project management. The key relationship is between the project manager and his or her client. The building blocks of this relationship include the project manager's professional competence, open and effective communications, a genuine interest in and understanding of the client and their business needs and the demonstrated behavior of always acting in the best interest of the client.

While the relationship originates as part of the project assignment, it is fostered by the project manager's willing commitment to the assignment. It is first and foremost a service-based relationship with a complementary ethical obligation to act professionally on behalf of the client. Project stakeholders have two key indicators to gauge the quality of their relationship with the project manager. First, are they being kept suitably involved in the project? And second, are they being kept properly informed about its status? My colleagues have written at length about the consulting skills that project managers should employ (Chapter 4), as well as the importance of building and engaging in a service-oriented mindset (Chapter 3).

6. Leading the Team

I purposely use the word "lead" rather than "manage" or "control." Leadership extends both the client's and the project manager's sphere of influence beyond the mere administration of a project. Leadership by the client ennobles the project's objective. It raises the stakes, legitimizes the need and changes the effort from a game to a cause.

One of the most powerful motivators for IT professionals is the opportunity to make a real difference in the business. It's truly regrettable that so few business clients fail to leverage this powerful secret to project success. On the other hand, leadership by the project manager emboldens the actions of the team. Project teams thrive on being allowed (or empowered) to be creative, to experience the excitement of discovery, to enjoy a sense of real accomplishment and to have fun while doing "great" things. Simply put, a good project manager can lead a project team to places it could never be driven to. We've discussed the qualities of leadership and how to make this transformation in Chapter 2.

One final point about motivation - motivation is not something a project manager "does" to a team member. Rather, it's something a team member does for him- or herself. Motivation is a door that is locked from the inside. The best a project manager can do is create a climate that enables and encourages good work. The vast majority of IT professionals I've met in my career want to do a good job. It's truly unfortunate that far too many of them are forced into situations that discourage, inhibit and on occasion penalize their best efforts. The key is to manipulate the environment, not the people.

7. CLOSE THE PROJECT

The last process in managing a project is to close and evaluate the project. The central activity of this process involves compiling lessons learned from the finished project and using them to form the basis of improvement recommendations. These improvements are directed at enhancing the enterprise's tools, methods and procedures for future projects. This cycle is the driving force behind the continuously learning organization.

The final act of a project manager is to officially end the project. Win, lose or draw, it's always good form to close down the effort on a gracious note – with a party if deserved, or a wake if warranted.

SECTION 5
The Four Tenets of the Project Manager's Mindset

Now that we've discussed the three-phase approach to managing projects, we can turn our attention to something that's a little less tangible but just as important: Changing our staff's mindset toward project management.

Being a successful project manager requires more than just following project management methodologies, approaches and metrics. It requires a fundamental change in the approach that most project managers take. If we allow our organizations to continue managing projects with their head in the wrong place, the chance of project success is nil. Here are four basic tenets that every project manager should internalize in order to get their head in the project management game, in order of priority.

Tenet 1:
Serve the Client

Being a project manager requires committing oneself to both the "letter and spirit" of the job. Project managers have typically been held to three accountabilities: "on time," "on budget" and "according to requirements." I regard these as the "letter" portion of the job title. In essence, they're what project managers are paid to do.

But there's a fourth and – from what I see, often forgotten – accountability: client service. I consider this the "spirit" of the job. As an agent of the client, the project manager's job is to provide service and to provide it professionally, competently and with the best interests of the client in mind. The aim of this tenet is client satisfaction. Technology may be the underlying mechanism, but it's not the purpose of the project. It is there to perform a job that the client needs to do.

So the number one job is serving the client by understanding their interests, their challenges, their relationships with others in the business, and their history. This requires a deft touch and a willingness to really listen and attempt to value the client's needs. After all, project managers can't provide good service if they don't know whom they're serving and why.

Some workshop participants have challenged me on this point by asserting that I must therefore believe that the client is always right. What I'm actually saying is that the client isn't always right, but they're always the client. Service requires giving respect and deference to the client's requirements and needs. At the same time, service is not servitude, and just doing everything the client says is not providing a service. These concepts are so important that we've covered the topic of improving our organizations' service mentality in Chapter 3.

Also, while the chief aim of this tenet is client satisfaction, the point isn't to achieve satisfaction at all costs. Sometimes, the greatest service you can perform for your client is to tell them that the current course of action is not in their best business interest, and to provide viable options. I refer to this as "adult dialogue," and it should be revered on a project. In other words, don't accept whining, moaning, excuses, lies, or finger pointing. If you like what is happening on the project, say so. If you don't like what's happening, say so. Be genuine. No baggage, no games, no bullying. Engage in "fear-free" communication. Insist on hearing and telling the plain and simple truth. Demand personal accountability for quality work by everyone on the project. It's interesting to speculate how many project failures could have been averted if only the project manager had engaged the client in real adult dialogue.

Of course, not all clients are ready for this two-way relationship. For instance, you might get a client who's not sufficiently knowledgeable or engaged. In this case, the project manager needs to educate them on their role and responsibilities, how crucial it is for them to provide strategic direction, help resolve political problems, make resources available, champion the cause to the enterprise, establish clear priorities – the things that only an executive sponsor can do. The project manager may also need to educate the client on his role, why it's crucial to do the upfront planning and structuring, to have a project charter, to engage in change management strategies, etc.

The challenge for project managers is to create the kind of relationship with the client that makes these types of exchanges realistic and credible – which is not always easy when the client has significantly more power in the organization than they do. Let's face it; one of the biggest challenges for project managers is to have so little authority but so much responsibility for making the project succeed. We talk more about this imbalance of power and how to navigate the resulting politics in Chapter 8 on managing politics.

TENET 2:
ACCOMPLISH THE MISSION

The second tenet revolves around the job of project management. Here's where the project manager brings his or her craft into play – all the work I described in Sections 2, 3 and 4, earlier in the chapter. This is the technical work of project management, and clients should have a solid expectation that the project manager working with them is strong in his or her craft.

It's important to note that all the mechanical work involved with accomplishing the mission is secondary to serving the client. It's easy to get lost in the weeds of project management methodologies and tools and lose your focus on what you're really doing.

TENET 3:
GROW THE TEAM

Note the use of the term "grow" rather than "develop." Nurturing a good team is not an engineering project in which you assemble parts and pieces according to a prescribed series of processes. It's more akin to agriculture, where you start with good seeds, put them in fertile soil, provide them with water and sunlight and – hopefully – get a good crop. But a good crop is not guaranteed; you can do all the right things, and the people you've assembled may still not gel as a team.

To maximize your chances, you need to make a conscious decision to work skillfully with the staff members you've selected. You need to solicit their ideas, create a collaborative environment and provide a forum in which their best efforts can surface. The best environment in which to grow a team is one that's open and invites project team members to elevate issues and concerns. Your goal should be that at the end of a project, the people who've worked together are better for it – they've learned new things, applied their specialties and shared their own worth and value with the enterprise.

Remember, people require lots of time. It's an oxymoron to believe that you can be efficient with the people on your project. Effectiveness as a project manager is born out of investing time in the wellbeing of the client, stakeholders and team members. Taking care of the troops is not just a military truism. I have often been amazed, inspired and even saved by the good works of my project team members. Take the time necessary to help ensure that your relationships with the people on your project are always in good repair. Then, be ruthlessly efficient with everything else.

You'll know you have a high-performance, "gelled" team when you see the following characteristics:

- A shared elevating vision or goal.

- A strong sense of team identity.

- Mutual trust.

- Interdependence among team members.

- Open and effective communications.

- A sense of autonomy.

- Low turnover.

- Joint ownership of the product.

- A high level of obvious enjoyment.

Of course, these are human beings we're talking about, and just like with raising kids, there are a limited number of ways to get it right and an infinite number of ways to get it wrong. That's why this third tenet is where many inexperienced project managers stumble, particularly with the increasing number of virtual teams, where members in different geographic regions meet via videoconferences and communicate via e-mail and phone. When team members never get the chance to meet, they may not even consider the importance of "gelling" and truly working as a team. They might easily adopt a contractor's mentality, where they get the work done and move on. That will be an ongoing challenge to project managers trying to instill a sense of teamwork.

Notice that "growing the team" comes after "accomplishing the mission." Getting the work done is the priority, of course, and there are times when the necessity and urgency of the work takes preeminence. But let's face it – no one wants to get the mission accomplished on the backs of a broken and mangled staff.

TENET 4:
OWN THE PROJECT

This last tenet is the enabler for all the others – the solid belief on the part of the project manager that he or she has a personal stake in the outcome of the project. I have come to regard project management as the courageous application of common sense in uncommon situations. But where does the courage come from if not from the genuine belief that our good name will be associated with the results of the project? The success or failure of the project reflects on the project manager, and that personal aspect is important. If the project manager doesn't have a sense that he or she is on the line – that the project doesn't reflect his or her talents and abilities – then they won't be able to make the hard calls that a project often demands.

For instance, without a strong personal stake in the project, how can you find the courage to tell a client that what he or she is doing is not in the best interests of the business? Or deal with a team member whose performance is below par? Or confront a vendor that's not doing its job? Without a sense of ownership, it's pretty easy to slough off responsibility, overlook shoddy work and dismiss dysfunctional behavior. The project manager's attempts at championing the project will ring hollow, and the team will see through it in a minute.

This strong personal identity with the project is not the same as the sponsor's ownership of the product. The sponsor truly owns the project deliverables because they paid for them. A personal sense of ownership by a project manager does not, in any way, absolve the client of their responsibilities as client.

It's also important to note that project managers' ownership should not be construed to mean that IT is taking over the project. Organizational sourcing of the project management role should have no affect on the professional obligation to act as the client's agent and not as their boss.

CONCLUSION: THINKING LIKE A PROJECT MANAGER

Project management is truly a blend of both art and science. But that's not widely understood in our industry. From what I see in companies throughout the U.S. today, IT professionals focus way too much on the tools, methodologies and other mechanical aspects of project management. And by going so far out there in the weeds, they often lose sight of why they're managing all these projects in the first place: to create systems that satisfy the real needs and requirements of the clients who depend on them.

I'm not saying that project managers don't need to know their craft. In fact, knowing the mechanics of structuring, planning and managing projects is absolutely essential, which is why I build workshops around these very important building blocks of the job.

However, managing a project is not a purely mechanical endeavor. The difference between project successes and failures is how those skills are applied, and the secret ingredient is the project manager's own mindset. When you overlay a solid understanding of project management essentials with a mindset of satisfying the client, that's a recipe for success.

It's really a matter of staying focused on these essentials and trying to avoid boiling the ocean. I had the unfortunate experience of working for a manager who constantly tried to do too much. Nothing was good enough. Every minor slip or shortfall was treated as a capital offense. He meddled, nagged, and bemoaned every action taken on the project. It was not only exhausting and highly unprofessional, but it was in large measure unnecessary to the success of the project. I believe there are just six areas of focus on most projects.

1. Pay attention to the schedule.

2. Mind the budget.

3. Manage the scope.

4. Monitor the quality.

5. Foster your relationship with your client.

6. Attend to your team.

That's pretty much it; most everything else is just noise.

In short, project managers won't succeed by memorizing the latest techniques and immersing themselves in the methodology of the day. It's a job that requires positive relationships and total engagement with people.

Tenets for Managing Projects

10. Manage the work, not the plan.

9. Deal only with reality – insist on seeing results, not just being told about them.

8. Projects don't go from great to awful overnight; it happens one day at a time.

7. Bad news doesn't age well. Keep your client, stakeholders, management, and team members informed.

6. MBWA – Manage By Wandering Around (with credit to Tom Peters, *In Search of Excellence*.) If you want to know what's going on, get up out of your cube and go look at it.

5. Be efficient with things but effective with people.

4. Pace is not the same as progress – provide time for people to catch their breath and celebrate their successes.

3. Stay focused; don't try to boil the ocean.

2. Insist on "adult behavior" from everyone on the project.

1. Earn the privilege to be regarded as the project manager every day.

SPECIFIC ACTIONS I WILL TAKE

✔

✔

✔

Sharpening Your
Political Savvy

8

Managing Projects–
The Science & the Art

6

Negotiating: Getting What You
Want without Damaging
the Relationship

5

Evolving into the
Role of Consultant

4

Building a Client–
Focused IT Cuture

3

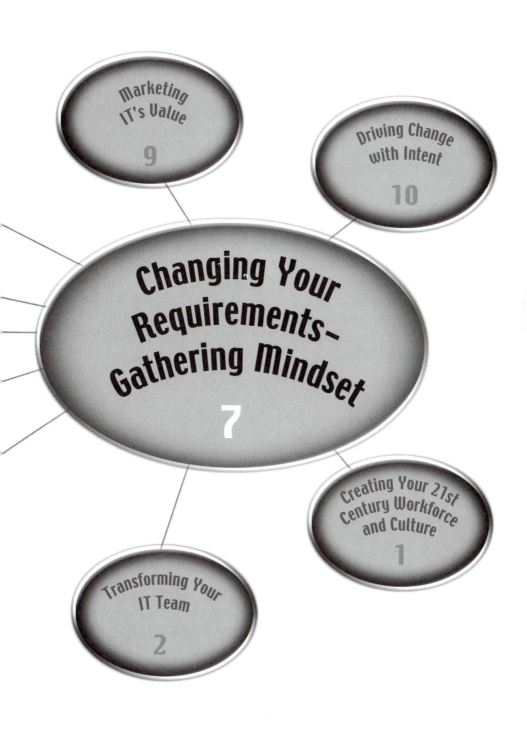

The success of any IT project is determined at the very beginning of the project lifecycle, when the IT staff meets with business clients to gather requirements. But IT's track record with this important phase is similar to its history with project management itself: abysmal. Requirements have been gathered for decades, but most IT organizations have yet to discover a consistently successful way of sitting down with business clients, discussing their needs and translating those needs into a useful system, enhancement, customization or software package selection.

In fact, according to some statistics, poor requirements gathering is the cause of about 70% of today's technology project failures. That's because passing along one bad requirement is akin to throwing a stone into a pond and watching how far the ripples go. According to some calculations, each badly defined requirement results in 10 bad design statements, which then can multiply out to 100 incorrect coding statements. Even if that's an exaggeration, you can easily see how poor requirements negatively impact application integrity, maintenance costs and client satisfaction. This is true whether you're looking to build a custom system, buy a new software package or enhance an existing system.

Skipping requirements gathering is like building a house without a plan. For instance, I've seen companies buy software that didn't meet their business needs, mainly because they wanted to save time on the requirements step. When they tried to modify the package to meet their needs, they found they didn't know the requirements. Sadly, they concluded that the step they skipped really did need to be done in order to make the package useful.

I often see organizations turn to yet another vendor tool or methodology in their attempt to improve this situation. But just like with project management, IT is facing a problem that requires less of a scientific fix and more of a mindset change – a change that emphasizes the upfront work of really communicating with business clients to discover what they need.

From what I've seen in my 24 years in the IT profession and from working with clients across the country, this is a mindset change that's way past due, as business leaders grow increasingly frustrated with the disconnect between what clients need and what IT delivers. I learned about the importance of good requirements throughout my varied IT career, which included stints in analysis, development, production support, project management and relationship management. It became clear to me that to have success in any of these roles, it all starts with good requirements. Everyone who has to read and use them appreciates them, they increase productivity and quality, and they add accountability. And lastly, a good requirement is measurable because either the end product delivers on that requirement, or it doesn't.

Specifically, I learned two critical things about gathering requirements:

1. Always figure out and then describe WHAT the problem is and always state WHAT is needed, because there are many solutions to a given problem.

2. Don't come up with a solution before you know what the requirements are. There are just too many people who want to tell you how to do your job.

How many times has your IT staff rushed through the client interview stage in order to jump into what they consider to be the "real work" of designing and programming? And when they do spend time with clients, are they really listening? Or are they busy trying to relate what they hear to something they're already familiar with, like another system they've recently built or a platform they're comfortable with? Other times, they might hear just a little bit and immediately determine that what clients want simply can't be done, instead of asking more questions to verify their understanding.

To better understand the problem, imagine you're a bridge designer, and a client comes to you, describing his need to get over a body of water in order to cross from one landmass to another separate piece of land. You'd start designing a bridge, right? Well, what if you were in the submarine business? Or the airline industry? Or a tunnel engineer? The point is, the client simply needs to get from one piece of land to the other, and whether that's best done by bridge, submarine, balloon or dirigible can only be determined by an unbiased third party who knows how to unlock the client's real needs and expectations. How many times a day does the client need to go back and forth? How quickly does he expect to be able to get there? How many other people need to do the same thing? Do they all have to move at the same time?

And it's not as though business clients are any better at this. In fact, today's more technology-savvy clientele often come to IT with a solution based on a recent article they've read or a conference they've attended. Then, the IT staff feels it's up to them to implement that solution rather than backing up and finding out what the client's real needs are.

No tool or methodology can resolve these problems. It's a matter of changing the IT organization's mindset and helping them develop new skills so they can see things through the eyes of the client, establish a rapport, ask the right questions, actively listen to the responses, ensure understanding and accurately translate those needs into a written document. And keep in mind that the ability to quickly and effectively capture, validate, and control client requirements doesn't just apply to project managers and business analysts. These are essential survival skills for anyone working in today's IT environment of lean staffing and crunch-mode projects.

When IT leaders become more aware of the skills gaps that exist in their own organizations, they can transform their organization's requirements-gathering culture and help individuals develop the needed skill sets, independent of any particular vendor's tool or methodology. When they affect this type of change, the results can be astounding. I know – I've seen it. Recently, I worked with a client who had two project teams that were trained to do requirements gathering. The first team adapted the techniques the second team did not. The first team delivered their project on time and on schedule, with high client satisfaction. Their clients, geographically dispersed, were enthusiastic about how well the project team understood their needs and communicated their progress. The second team was over budget, behind schedule and constantly heard complaints from their clients. To paraphrase one of the client responses, "We don't know what we're getting or when."

SECTION 1

The "What," Not the "How"

I think of the requirements-gathering process as a journey, with plenty of precarious twists and unexpected turns along the way. If you're a skillful driver, you can stay on track and arrive at your destination. But poorly negotiating the curves or taking a wrong turn can result in a lot of wandering along unpaved roads that lead nowhere. Unfortunately, a successful arrival requires a skill set that – from what I've seen in my work with IT organizations – most IT professionals don't have. It's the job of the IT leader to not only become familiar with the optimum route to requirements-gathering success but also to teach their staffs how to navigate.

The first and most important skill is steering the client interview toward what I call the "what," not the "how." From the hundreds of projects I've worked on, I can say that this is the biggest downfall of most IT professionals. In their zeal to get to what they consider "real IT work," many project managers and business analysts start shaping the solution to the client's needs (the "how") before they really understand what those needs are in the first place (the "what"). But as soon as they do this, it's a guarantee that they're veering from the right path.

Let me explain it this way. Do you have any 8- to 12-year-olds in your life – a neighbor, a niece or nephew, a son or daughter? If so, you may have heard them say how much they need, really need, a cell phone. But have you ever asked them what they intend to do with this electronic device they seemingly can't live without? If so, you've probably heard answers like, "Talk to my friends" (have you ever been on the other end of an 8-year-old's phone conversation?) "Let my parents know where I am" (how far do 10-year-olds really travel these days?) or more likely, "Download a cool ring tone." By pressing further, you might uncover that it's not really a cell phone your young tweener friend really needs at all and that what he or she is really after is a sense of independence, of feeling like a grown-up, of keeping up with the latest technology rage – all things that can be achieved in a variety of ways and not necessarily with a cell phone (which they're bound to lose or at least lose interest in after showing it off for a few days).

Thankfully, talking with clients is usually not like talking with a 12-year-old, but the common thread is that you can't automatically assume that the solution clients say they need is really the optimum one. Arriving at that requires digging underneath the surface, steering the client toward describing not "how" they want something built but "what" they need to accomplish. Remember, your goal is to figure out what the client needs from the new system or modification or software package – not how he or she wants it to be built or designed. In other words, project managers, business analysts and others need to learn to leave the "how" to the designers and consider their job to be getting to the "what."

To understand this better, let's go back to the bridge example. If someone comes up to you and says, "There's a river over there; can you build me a bridge?" that's a "how." But if you ask the person, "What do you need to do? What is your goal?" they might answer, "I need to get to the other side." That's the "what." And when you get to the what, you realize there are many options for the "how," whether it's a bridge, a tunnel, a ferry or a submarine. In other words, you don't want to design the answer; you just want them to express what they need to do. There can be many solutions and many designs to fit the client's needs, and that should be left to the designers to figure out, not the requirements gatherers.

By asking "what" rather than short-circuiting the process by starting with the "how," you can air out many other designs and approaches, some of which might be better than the "how" the client comes to you with.

A typical example from my experience is a client bringing me a screen or a report with a new column added and saying, "This is what I want!" By questioning "what" the client needs with the column, I might find that the information is derived; for instance, formulas need to be defined, the data doesn't exist anywhere in IT (it's on a client's spreadsheet), or the information is readily available somewhere else, like in another report or application not currently used by the client.

I was working with an IT organization that related the following example of falling into the "how" trap. Their business client came to them with modified screenshots showing how they needed the system to be changed. The IT organization worked with the client to spec out the changes and sent it offshore for development. When the newly modified screens were returned for testing, someone in the IT organization asked why a new set of screens was developed to handle functionality that already existed! It turns out that the business client was unaware that the functionality existed, and the existing functionality would work just fine.

SECTION 2

The Importance of the Interview

The next fork in the road that can throw requirements-gatherers off-course is the mistake of taking client requests at face value. Far too many IT organizations take on the role of order-taker – listening to what clients want and unquestioningly delivering to spec – only to discover the final result doesn't serve the business needs at all. This is such an easy trap for IT professionals to fall into, that we discuss it in more depth in Chapter 4 on consulting skills.

Simply put, clients don't always know how to communicate their needs, and it's now up to IT to lead the way. And the way to do that is by developing strong interview skills, which is yet another Achilles' heel for many IT professionals. From what I see in the IT organizations I work with, most IT staffs approach the client interview as a check-off item to complete as quickly as possible rather than as an opportunity to build rapport, establish a partnership and really understand what the business is trying to accomplish. It's the IT leader's job to sensitize the IT staff to the importance of the interview and teach them how to take advantage of this prime time with the client.

Good interviews don't just happen. It's good to ask a lot of questions, but you don't want to come across as disrespectful or annoying. It's important to steer the client toward talking about "what" he wants, but you don't want to appear arrogant or negative. There are many fine lines that need to be walked, and the only way for the IT staff to keep its balance is to develop communication skills.

One of the most common interview problems I see is when the interviewer becomes frustrated with the interviewee, especially when he thinks the interviewee doesn't know anything. I have heard statements such as, "Can I talk to X, who knows something about the request/problem," without realizing that they have just insulted the person they are addressing (usually management).

First and foremost, a satisfying interview requires establishing a rapport with the person or people with whom you're partnering, which means allowing the conversation to naturally flow beyond a discussion of work and technology. Such camaraderie will go far when you inevitably run into conflicts, confrontations and other difficult conversations with the client in the future. The idea of establishing rapport is so important that we've also discussed it in Chapter 4 on consulting skills and Chapter 8 on politics.

For the purposes of requirements gathering, however, there are some specific ways to open the lines of communication. One idea is to encourage the IT organization to conduct their interviews in the client's office, which will help set the client at ease. This is important because an intimidated or defensive client won't be inclined to open up to the requirements-gatherer. This also gives the IT professional the chance to look around the office for personal mementos such as photographs that reveal something about the client's personality or life outside of work. These are easy conversation starters that can encourage a natural flow of communication that will benefit the IT staff when it gets down to the business at hand.

Because it doesn't come easily to many IT professionals, they need to be encouraged to ask about the client's golf game, his white-water rafting trip, her marathon training and listen for interests that they share. Such tidbits can be used for further conversation-starters when IT professionals see the client again in the hallway or at their next meeting. Most people enjoy talking about themselves to people who seem truly interested, and that's what establishes human connections.

And last but not least, it is estimated that 55% of communication is non-verbal. I remember being in a client's office when IT called to get some information. The client said "OK" but rolled their eyes, frowned and let out a groan. The caller heard, "OK," but to anyone present in the office, there was obviously an issue that needed to be discussed and resolved.

Do note, though, that if an individual on the IT staff doesn't feel capable of engaging in this type of rapport, it's probably better for them to try another tack, like talking about the weather or something else of general human interest. The last thing you want is for them to come across as a phony that ritualistically asks the same question about the same photograph with no genuine interest in the client's answers. Similarly, if the client's office reflects nothing personal, that should be taken as a cue to the person's more bottom-line-oriented personality, in which case the IT staff should stick to the business at hand, such as asking, "How are sales?" or, How's business?"

Another common interview mistake is for requirements gatherers to fail to establish a common language between themselves and the client. IT needs to be sensitized to the fact that there is, indeed, a difference in terminology in the two worlds, and second, they need to be proactively encouraged to adopt the terminology of the business client. They can't be too proud to ask for definitions – acronyms in one industry can mean something else entirely in another industry, or even in another division of the same company! Problems occur when you persist in using the jargon of your own world or when you assume you understand the client's terminology.

In fact, you may discover that different business clients are using different words to mean the same thing. In those cases, the IT staff can serve as a bridge between clients, encouraging them to agree to a uniform vocabulary for a particular project or initiative and clearly defining that vocabulary in a project glossary or dictionary. When everyone is on the same page with their terminology, it eliminates a lot of room for confusion.

I have also come across the same acronym that means two different things depending on which business area of the company I'm working with. Since IT deals with the entire company, this leads to confusion when team members change, or requirements are passed onto designers. Not to mention the issues it causes for new hires, contractors and offshore developers.

Here are some additional tips on helping the IT organization improve its interview success:

- **Take a who/what inventory.** Chances are that multiple clients will need to be interviewed, so it would be wise for the requirements gatherer to do some research ahead of time as to what pieces of information they need and who's the most likely source for that information. For each person they interview, they should know their objective. They don't, for instance, want to waste someone's time talking about general ledger concerns if that's not their area of work.

- **Make a written list of questions.** This will help the requirements gatherer manage their time during the interview. They may arrive with 10 questions, but if the person turns out to be a treasure trove of information, it might take half an hour to get the answer to the first one. If they still have nine to go, they can determine, in partnership with the client, whether they want to move on or plan another meeting.

- **Stay in "ask" mode.** If the requirements gatherer concentrates on asking questions rather than making statements or not responding at all, they'll avoid two common errors that I see IT professionals make: making assumptions and forming arguments. If they have even a shadow of a doubt about whether they understand something, they should ask for clarification or otherwise check their understanding. It's better to play stupid than misunderstand. And if they don't agree with something the client says, they should respond with a question. They're not there to argue; they're there to find out what the client needs.

- **Provide prototypes.** A good way to verify mutual understanding is to use visual aids, such as mock screens, reports or models. It's important for the requirements gatherer to emphasize to the client, however, that the prototype is not the end product and is simply a tool to ensure everyone's on the same page. Too often, when the IT staff draws a mock screen, the client is surprised when the actual screen doesn't turn out that way. One way to avoid this is to never leave the prototypes behind with the client.

- **Craft a smooth ending.** When ending the interview, the requirements gatherer should make sure they recap their understanding of what they heard in the interview, explain the next steps and express appreciation for the person's time.

SECTION 3
Communicating through Pictures

A third wrong turn that I often see IT professionals make along the requirements-gathering path is to begin writing up the requirements before ensuring that they and the client are on the same page. All too often, after the client interview, the requirements-gatherer disappears, sometimes for weeks, writes up the requirements and then presents a fully written document to the client for feedback. When the client finally gets back to the IT professional – usually after a lengthy time lag – with changes, the process repeats itself, stretching out the back-and-forth review period for several months, with many lengthy lulls. At one company, requirements documents get rewritten an average of seven times before they reach final-copy stage! This approach is time-consuming and absurd, and in the end, the chances of getting it right are slim to none.

Note that this is not what an iterative approach should look like. A healthy iteration means the work is being done, reviewed with users and quickly corrected in hours or days and repeated until the document is correct or complete. That's different from writing a full-length document, publishing it and tweaking it over a period of months.

To achieve that, I suggest inserting a picture-drawing phase into the process before jumping into the document-writing phase. Call them models, context diagrams, event analyses or anything you wish – the idea is to create a clear communication tool that's easy for both IT and the client to see how everything connects and what's in and out of scope.

I've seen this method work on numerous occasions. In one case, a senior IT vice president had bought a software package to replace an existing antiquated application. He thought it solved the business needs and would be easy to install. There were no requirements. The development team was certain that the project would be a failure but was unable to communicate that upward.

Within an hour, we drew a context diagram to show all the system interfaces that needed to be developed to communicate with the new package. There were 57 system interfaces that would need to be designed, developed and tested, and this did not include installing the package, loading the data or ensuring the package met the client's needs.

Two hours later, after reviewing the context diagram, the senior VP cancelled the project, saying he didn't realize how big an effort it was to install and that we would need to get the requirements done before purchasing a new package. A picture on one page communicated what the developers had been trying to tell management for two months!

In another case, I was involved in a large IT effort to build a new regulatory business process. We used modeling to first define the existing processes, and then modified the existing processes to accommodate the new process.

The first day was difficult, as the clients couldn't understand why we were drawing pictures and not writing requirements. But by day 2, they had begun to fully utilize the modeling approach, with comments such as, "Take process X, modify this, this and this, and it will do what we need to do." We were also able to establish and document a common business language definition.

Because most people can draw or model more quickly than they can write, this new step effectively minimizes the lull between initial interviews and the feedback loop, which keeps the discussion fresh and as close to real-time as possible. Additionally, most people are more responsive to pictures and diagrams than a wordy document, which makes it easier to pull clients into a two-way, engaging conversation vs. the arm's-length, removed and disconnected type of communication that written documents promote.

Diagrams also make it easier for clients to see and explain what's wrong or missing in the system or process IT has modeled vs. long written documents. In fact, with longer documents, by the time many clients and IT staff get partway through them; they can barely remember what they read in the first half. But with a picture, IT can walk through the diagram with the client and discuss what's right and wrong.

If the IT staff does a good job with the initial interview and the iterations that follow from the picture-drawing stage, they'll find that when they actually write the requirements document, they'll end up revising it once or twice at most. That's because everybody involved has bought into the ideas and thoughts behind the document, used a common language and have given their feedback upfront.

A word of warning: You may see so much success with picture-drawing that you're tempted to go right to the prototyping phase, without writing a requirements document, or perhaps writing requirements only for business logic. However, this is a dangerous approach. While I have seen IT management push the idea of skipping written requirements, the risk is significant. Consider how vulnerable you'd be if key staff left the organization due to turnover, or a decision is made to offshore development. The lack of written requirements is a production support nightmare, not to mention when enhancements are requested. In addition, without an agreed upon set of requirements, there is no baseline established to manage change.

SECTION 4

Writing a Solid Requirements Document

As we near the end of the requirements-gathering journey, there's still another fork in the road that can throw IT professionals off the path: writing the actual requirements document. Let's go back to the points made at the very beginning of this chapter. Since requirements are what designers use to design, testers use to test, etc., one mistake in the requirements document has a negative ripple effect, plus we end up delivering something that doesn't fill the client's needs. We end up with patchwork new applications, with a high level of post-implementation defects, low client satisfaction, requests for enhancements, budget and schedule overruns – and that's if we succeed!

The goal is to write a simple document that is clear and concise. It should be easily understood by IT and the business, from senior management to staff, with no ambiguity. I once worked for a CIO who said, "If I can understand it, then you've done a great job of writing the requirements." In other words, write it for someone who doesn't know what needs to be done.

So, in writing the requirements document, it's important to hold the power of words in the highest esteem, especially with something that requires the language precision that requirements documents do. This is where the rubber meets the road, and it's important for requirements writers to be as accurate as they possibly can, which again requires learning some new skills, this time based around written communications.

There are several language tricks you can pass along to requirements writers to ensure precision in the document. Here are two:

The power of "MUST." One is to make ample use of the word "must." "Must" is one of the most powerful words in the English language, because when we use it, there are no two ways about the statement you're making. "X must do Y," plain and simple, 100% of the time, no exceptions. It's not the same with words like "should" and "shall," which imply there's an undefined "maybe" out there, an unnamed exception to the rule. Those grey areas are exactly what lead writers of requirements documents into trouble.

Unlike its cousins "should" and "shall," "must" exposes the exceptions and forces people to define them. When clients read a "must" statement, they're likely to respond, "No, actually, that shouldn't happen under these specific conditions." This helps us capture what's so easy to miss – the exceptions to the rule.

It's just a fact of life that many times, when you say, "X must do Y," someone will find an exception, even if it's as hidden as, "except when there's a blue moon following the harvest moon on the fifth month of an odd year." And those are the things that all too often just don't make it into the code.

Here's an example. At one company, a project team wrote a document with zero defects traced back to the requirements phase. That's because through computer modeling, 37 defects were exposed, all of which were instances in which each "shall" was changed to a "must." When these changes were brought to the client, eight statements were flagged as having multiple exceptions.

Watch out for "AND." Another word to watch is "and." As much as you can, try to eliminate any stray "ands" from your document, because their presence indicates that you've combined two thoughts that should be separate from each other. The whole idea is to keep the statements simple, and when it comes to designing code for the statements, it will be much easier if the designer understands there are two distinct thoughts, not two thoughts rolled into one.

Requirements need to be expressed in short, simple sentences with their associated exceptions. Way too often, I see one-sentence paragraphs that describe multiple requirements, which confuses everyone involved.

Conclusion

If IT professionals want to improve their project success rate, the first place to look is at the very beginning of the project lifecycle: the requirements-gathering phase. This is not a phase to speed through and check off as soon as possible; it's an opportunity to establish a partnering relationship with the client and use all the communication skills you can muster to truly understand what the client needs.

For years, organizations have tried and failed to improve their requirements-gathering process, using the new tools being promoted or the methodology of the day. But despite all their efforts, they find themselves running into the same brick wall, falling down and wondering yet again why they can't get it right.

That's why some IT leaders are beginning to try something different. They're setting upon the path of establishing a new mindset among their organizations to approach their projects differently and embark on the requirements-gathering journey with their compasses pointed in the right direction. With the right skills in hand, they can navigate the winding path and take all the right turns.

When you help your staff grow their communication and interpersonal skills, they become more insightful interviewers. It's only then that IT will stop building expensive bridges to nowhere and start helping their clients walk on water.

Techniques for Changing Your Requirements–Gathering Mindset

10. Establish rapport.

9. Communication is the key.

8. Interview the right people.

7. Talk in the business language and use pictures (models).

6. Don't assume - ask.

5. Don't solve the "problem" before you know WHAT it is.

4. Requirements are short, concise sentences.

3. Use the power of MUST - exceptions will kill you.

2. WHAT is a requirement, not HOW.

1. Give the people WHAT they want.

SPECIFIC ACTIONS I WILL TAKE

✔

✔

✔

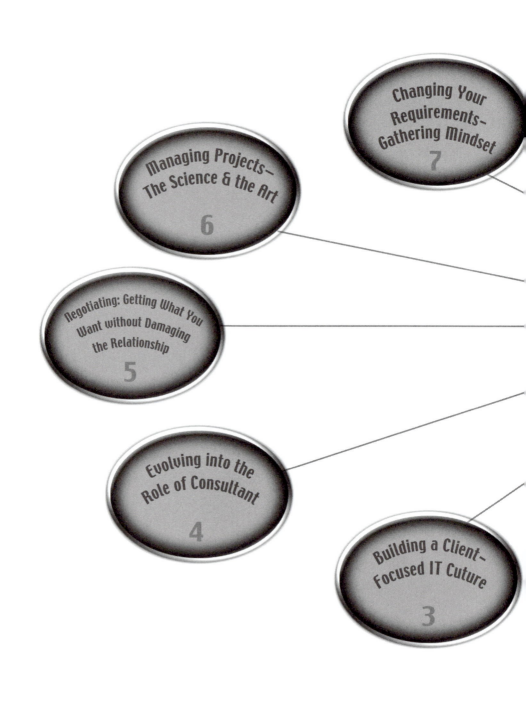

Changing Your
Requirements–
Gathering Mindset

7

Managing Projects–
The Science & the Art

6

Negotiating: Getting What You
Want without Damaging
the Relationship

5

Evolving into the
Role of Consultant

4

Building a Client–
Focused IT Cuture

3

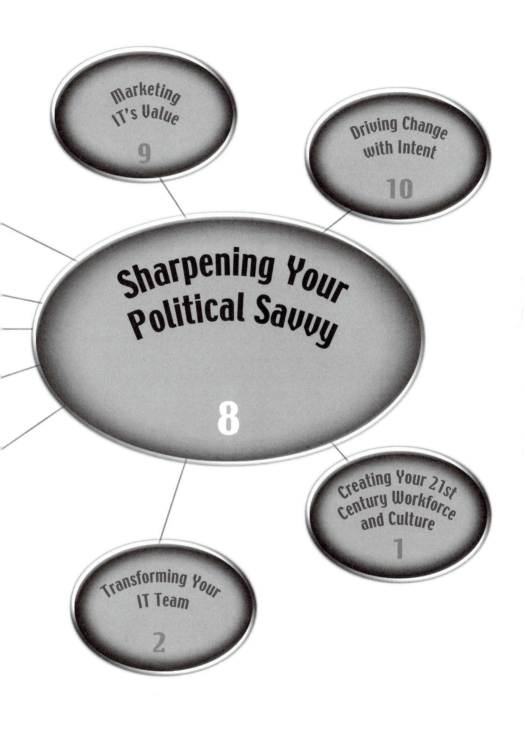

Marketing
IT's Value

9

Driving Change
with Intent

10

Sharpening Your
Political Savvy

8

Creating Your 21st
Century Workforce
and Culture

1

Transforming Your
IT Team

2

Many IT professionals view politics as something nasty. They'd rather resist, avoid or ignore politics all together. Intrigue, power plays, control tactics, conflict – what does this have to do with managing technology? "Who me?" you might hear an IT professional say. "Leave it to others to battle for control and struggle for power. My job is to implement the technology solution."

But the fact is, where there's technology, there's change, and where there's change, there will be people who perceive themselves as winners and as losers. That's where politics begin. So, you can bury your head in the sand and ignore politics – and then you won't have to watch IT projects, the organization's reputation and your own career go down the drain! The plain truth is, corporate politics aren't just for business clients anymore.

But they never really were. In fact, whether you've been aware of it or not, navigating politics has been a required skill for IT professionals – and particularly for project managers – ever since this field became a viable profession. And I should know – I've got the scars to prove it. I spent many years managing IT projects during my career. As a project manager, I found myself ensnared in more politically charged situations than I care to admit. I encountered resistance from business clients who were suspicious about the changes being forced upon them. I was embroiled in power struggles between departments. I failed to get support from people I didn't even know were key to my project. I was robbed of resources by others higher up the organizational food chain who inserted their pet projects ahead of my own. My projects were getting hurt, and so was my reputation as a project manager.

My excuse for the project problems was that they were "politics" – and politics wasn't my job. But standing by helplessly while my projects were derailed was frustrating for me and damaging to my future. Saying it wasn't my fault was not an effective promotion strategy!

And the plain truth is that it was my fault. Not because I created the political problems, but because I did nothing to manage them. Admittedly, I wasn't the fastest learner, but over time, I realized I couldn't afford to stand by helplessly. Reluctant clients, warring business departments, unsupportive higher-ups – these things were creating serious wounds that could kill my career. I eventually realized I could deal with all of these factors if I paid attention to the political influences around me. So I got my head out of the sand and worked to understand project politics and improve my own political skills.

Having learned a few things the hard way, I created the Politics of IT Project Management workshop for O&A five years ago. I thought I could help other project managers avoid some of the bruises I got in the "School of Hard

Knocks." At the time, nothing like it existed, despite the fact that becoming politically savvy is absolutely essential to succeeding in this profession.

While political savvy is an essential skill for all levels of the IT organization, it's particularly crucial for project managers. Project managers have no authority over the business clients they work with, but they have plenty of responsibility to shepherd projects to completion. So in lieu of positional power, project managers need to learn the art of persuasion, influence, trust building and rapport – in essence, political skills – to get the resources they need.

Unfortunately, resources are scarce in any corporation. Even in good times, there's never enough money, time and people to do everything everyone wants to do. That means we're in competition with others for the resources we need to successfully complete our projects. Competition leads to internal conflicts. And since most corporations don't have thorough procedures to rationally allocate resources, the two means for resolving those conflicts are negotiations (discussed in Chapter 5) and politics.

So what is politics, anyway? Used negatively, politics is "intrigue or maneuvering within a group in order to gain control or power." You know it when you see it: It's the business client who just won't show up at your meetings. It's the divisional manager who refuses to accept the new corporate-standard accounting system. It's the sales department that insists it should have a major say in the development of the new procurement system. Negative politics divides people and disrupts progress.

But when used in a positive way, politics can bring people closer together. Positive politics is a legitimate activity to allow people with different interests to work out a collective purpose – and then work together to make it happen.

SECTION 1

Picturing Yourself as a Political Player

To play politics, IT professionals need to see themselves as political players. But many IT professionals don't have a clear picture of what it means to be politically savvy. So it might be easier to picture yourself navigating through a political situation outside of work. Consider this situation: You dropped off the lunch your child forgot to take to school this morning, and you see vending machines full of junk food around the cafeteria. Maybe you think the school's food policy should be changed to encourage healthier eating habits. What would be the first action you'd take? Would you storm into the principal's office and tell her she should be taking better care of the students?

More likely, you'd check with some teachers you've come to trust, to understand the history surrounding the development of the school's food policy. How long has it been there, and has anyone tried to change it before? Perhaps you'd talk with other parents first to gauge their reaction to your concerns. Maybe you'd even drum up some support and even excitement around the issue. Is there a school newsletter, local newspaper or parent blog? Maybe you'd get people discussing these issues through one of those media outlets.

You might even engage in some detective work: What are other schools doing about these issues? How long has the principal worked at this particular school, and what has been her previous reaction to suggested change? Does the principal prefer to talk by phone, email or meet face-to-face? Is there a group of teachers that seems to influence the principal more than others?

Clearly, your best chance to change things is through discovering the invisible influences – the internal politics – in the organization, and then playing your cards with those forces in mind.

And that's as true for the workplace as it is in a school, a neighborhood, or a volunteer organization. Where there are people – particularly people who sense that their stability, their beliefs and their overall security are at stake – there are politics. And where there is a technology initiative, there is change – change that will enflame those politics like a spark ignites gasoline.

SECTION 2

IT and Politics: Historically Strange Bedfellows

My brother-in-law managed a large sales territory for his company for 30 years. Harry knew that political savvy and awareness was critical to sales success. Any sales manager, vice president of finance or divisional manager will tell you that – they grow up understanding it through their entire corporate lives.

That's one of the biggest problems IT professionals have – everyone else in the corporation understands this stuff, and they've been left out of the loop. Worse, business people can't even fathom that IT doesn't consider corporate politics and are left to wonder why they're handling these everyday situations so badly. When I told Harry I was developing a workshop to help project managers understand politics, he was surprised. "Why wouldn't they know that stuff already?" he questioned. Because nobody told them it was important! Think of all the training you've had on your way to becoming an IT leader – did anyone warn you to look over your shoulder for the political problems technology projects might ignite, let alone coach you on how to proactively ensure they don't flare out of control?

It's easy to believe that because technology projects are designed to improve work processes that everyone in the company will happily jump on-board. But the reality is, technology projects always mean change, which is a threat to the status quo. As a result, there will always be a group of people who consider themselves the "winners," as well as their counterparts, who perceive themselves as the "losers." And while the "winners" make natural allies of IT and can be our best project champions, the "losers" will do everything they can to preserve and protect their territory. Unfortunately, those actions, either directly or inadvertently, could very well sabotage the project.

This is particularly true on the highly strategic, cross-divisional and even global projects that many companies are embarking on today. More and more projects are being launched with the intent of breaking down traditional silos and creating synergies among disparate parts of the business. In fact, it's fair to say that the degree of damaging politics that IT professionals can expect to encounter is in direct correlation with the visibility of the project and the variety of stakeholders involved.

In my project manager days, I was once approached by the CFO of a fast-growing company that had recently acquired several other businesses. He had a problem: With all the different financial systems in use, it was taking six weeks to close the books. The CFO wanted to standardize on a single application to improve speed and efficiency.

We set up a project team and worked with the corporate financial group to choose the right application and began testing it. Everything went so well that the CFO wanted to immediately install the new system in the first field division.

When I walked into the general manager's office of the targeted field division, I was shocked when the manager was less than pleased to see me. "We've heard what you've been doing at corporate," the general manager barked, "and I don't know why you even bothered coming out here. We run our business our way, and we've got a guarantee of autonomy directly from the CFO. Our financial system works just fine for us, and we're not going to change it."

I was a victim of politics, right? But it didn't have to be that way. What if, instead of being blind-sided, I had looked at the big picture before even agreeing to take on the project? Shouldn't I have considered the needs, goals and desires of the key stakeholders, in this case, the general managers of the field divisions? What if I had asked the CFO whether everyone was on-board with the standardization effort – instead of assuming that they'd be fine with all the changes it entailed, not to mention the loss of some of their autonomy? Then perhaps I could have said that I'd be happy to lead this system change after the CFO had taken the appropriate organizational readiness steps. And if the CFO was unwilling to do that, it would have been a real clue of the political hot water that awaited me.

Very likely, the CFO knew exactly what he was doing – putting IT into the position of playing the bad guy that forces conformance through a system change rather than the CFO doing it himself. It's often a rude awakening for IT professionals to discover that the "C" in a C-level position doesn't always stand for organization-wide "clout."

Clearly, career success will come to those who stop blaming politics and start handling them. Using politics as an excuse will no longer cut it when it comes to advancing the reputation and effectiveness of IT.

Politically savvy project managers can:

- Have their projects bumped up on the priority list.

- Cut through red tape.

- Receive greater recognition.

- Get management "buy-in" on their projects.

- Garner more project budget.

- Get the people they need – when they need them.

- Have their ideas heard.

- Bring projects to successful conclusions.

SECTION 3

A Five-Step Process for Developing Political Awareness

Once you accept that corporate politics are a given, you can strategize on how to personally navigate them, as well as teach your staff to become more politically savvy. This isn't a one-step process; rather a five-step roadmap that has helped numerous clients become more aware of the politics waiting to ensnare them and how to proactively avoid them.

1. Start Your Radar

The first step is getting outside the world of IT and taking an assessment of the people the project will affect. Who are the key stakeholders – the people most impacted by the project – and what are their connections, relationships and previous histories with each other? Beyond the obvious stakeholders, who are the people who believe they should have some say in the project? You need to enlarge your radar screen and not only track but also feel accountable for knowing the people who will be impacted by the project.

In order to do that, you have to become adept at ferreting out information that lives not in the world of facts but in the hidden world of rumor, innuendo and personal relationships. After all, projects are more about people than technology, and when people come together on projects, they arrive with a whole set of feelings, experiences, goals and prejudices that you need to understand.

IT professionals may not be accustomed to paying attention to those things. In order to accomplish their mantra of "on time, on budget, on spec," they actually might consider it noble to ignore the rumor and innuendo that seems to accompany every project they embark on – keep your hands clean and "stick to the facts, ma'am." After all, if you follow logic and make rational decisions based on known facts, isn't that the safest way to an optimal solution?

Unfortunately, the answer is no. Although many IT professionals might like to see the world as a giant problem just waiting to be solved, that approach doesn't account for human feelings, desires and struggles for power.

To understand the factors that influence our projects, IT professionals need to get to know key stakeholders on a more personal level. You don't need to become close buddies, but you do need to know people well enough to predict their behavior – where they'll form alliances, who their enemies are, who they won't cooperate with, who they're likely to gang up on. Imagine how much more smoothly things would go if you had a better handle on these factors that you might otherwise feel are outside of your control.

2. Determine Where the Power Bases Are

One of the key things to understand about project stakeholders is the clout they have in the organization. Clout has two dimensions: positional authority, which is where people stand on the corporate ladder, and influence, which is the power they yield outside of the organizational chart. People who are highly placed on both dimensions are the obvious movers and shakers to who project managers need to pay attention. It's possible, though to be influential without high positional authority. There are people who have hidden clout, and it's important to understand who they are, too.

Think back to the television show *M*A*S*H* – Radar is a good example of someone with hidden clout, despite being low in rank. Many administrative assistants are also people who yield a great deal of influence that could help or hinder you; particularly as they might control access to the people you need to get to know.

Understanding how people influence others is essential to the IT professional of the future, so we cover the topic further in Chapter 4 on consulting skills.

3. SORT YOUR ENEMIES FROM YOUR ALLIES

Don't fall into the naïve trap of believing that because you and your project sponsor are excited about the project that everyone is. You need to do some stakeholder analysis to figure out who stands to win and lose from the project – or who perceives themselves as winners or losers. From this analysis, you can predict who your allies and enemies will be, as well as who will ally with or oppose one another.

How people align themselves within a project depends on two key factors. The first is the degree to which they share common interests or WIIFMs on the project (we introduce this acronym in the introduction to the book). Second is the quality of the relationships they have with each other.

People who share common WIIFMs and who get along well are natural allies. Those who don't get along and who have opposing WIIFMs will be enemies on the project. In between are people who might overlook a bad relationship to ally with those who can help them get their WIIFMs, and people who like each other but can't see eye-to-eye on what they'll get out of the project.

By considering the positions of key players on a project, project managers can develop strategies to move people toward alliance through building strong relationships or promoting shared interests. Where enemies are so strong they can't be moved to less dangerous positions, strategies need to be made to contain potentially damaging behaviors.

4. Predict the Political Pitfalls, and Chart the Course

From the information you glean in steps 1-3, you should be able to predict what might happen from a political perspective on your project. These are the potential political pitfalls you might encounter. What kinds of actions might people take that would be harmful to the project? If someone thinks they stand to lose something and has an influential ally who doesn't like your boss, what might they do to undermine the project?

This process is a kind of risk analysis on a project, but instead of considering the technology risks, you're uncovering the political ones. Once you predict the pitfalls, you can determine what you can do to head off unfortunate events. We discuss the concept of clearing the path for change in Chapter 10.

5. Stay the Course

The last step is an ongoing one. You have to pay as much attention to your political course as you do to the traditional project plan. If your planned tactics don't work, you need to take corrective action. If a major change happens – like the appointment of a new project sponsor – it would be politically irresponsible to assume the person will have the same priorities as the previous sponsor. And if you find out they don't, you have to restructure your project, not resist the new sponsor's ideas and wish things were different.

For instance, I once led an IT team working on a highly visible, multi-year, multi-million dollar implementation of a major financial system. A couple of years into the project, which was going well, the CFO who'd been the project sponsor was promoted and replaced by another CFO.

I quickly got on the new CFO's calendar, thanks to the rapport I'd established with the CFO's administrator, and invited my boss, the CIO, to the meeting. I started the meeting with a recap of the project and how well it was going. Halfway through my presentation, the CFO pushed back his chair from the desk and stood up, saying, "This is a lot of bull – we're not going to continue with this project."

I confess I was speechless, but the CIO reacted immediately. "What do you mean we're not going to continue?" she said. "We're heading into year three of this project and have already spent more than half of the projected budget – we can't just throw that away!"

Not surprisingly, the CFO didn't take kindly to this retort. "Who are you to tell me what I can and can't do?" he said.

In less than five minutes, the relationship between IT and an important project sponsor was destroyed. Even though the CIO knew better, she was so personally invested in her own perspective that she lost sight of what the meeting was really about: bolstering an important relationship.

If the CIO had probed for more information, she would have found out that the CFO had a terrible experience with the system at his previous employer. Right or wrong, it was his prerogative to end the project. Instead of seeing it as wasting money and a lot of hard work, he may have viewed it as not throwing good money after bad. It then becomes IT's job to figure out how to shut down the project expediently and begin focusing on the next steps.

In retrospect, both the CIO and I should have entered the meeting with a better sense of who the CFO was and where he'd come from to better anticipate his reaction. If we weren't caught by surprise, we would have stood a better chance of thinking through our reactions – and not committing political suicide. You can read more about how to navigate these types of tough negotiations in Chapter 5.

SECTION 4
Developing Political Skills

Becoming politically savvy doesn't come naturally. IT leaders need to develop skills – both personally and among their staffs, especially among project managers – that will increase political awareness and make the IT organization successful at navigating politically churned-up waters. Here are some of the key skills required.

CREATIVITY

In order to widen your radar and assess the power bases among a project's key stakeholders (steps 1 through 3), you need to talk with people in the business, and not just at status meetings. This means finding creative ways of putting yourself in places where you'll interact with people socially. Some IT professionals I work with contend that "water cooler conversations" are a waste of time, but it's during these informal encounters that we can build the alliances that enable us to probe for more important information.

But that doesn't mean coming across like a CIA agent. Rather, IT professionals need to encourage informal conversations on topics outside of work – sports, kids, TV shows. These encounters will naturally help them become privy to the information they ultimately want to know, like the history of their business clients' inter-relationships.

Grabbing lunch together is a good way to do this. Everyone else in the business except IT "does lunch," and when IT professionals do go out for lunch, it's usually with someone else from IT rather than people important to our projects. But lunch is a great place to meet on neutral ground and probe for information that can be crucial to the project.

The key is to pay attention when people are talking to you or even around you. These informal encounters can be extremely valuable in improving your understanding of your business clients, increasing your empathy and sharpening your predictions on how they might react to project implications. No longer can we shut out the conversations around us – there's gold in all that noise.

INTERPERSONAL EFFECTIVENESS

Because IT focuses so heavily on producing deliverables within constrained schedules and budgets, it's easy to lose focus on the importance of interpersonal relationships. Consider that in sales, the whole focus is on relationships – salespeople operate from the core belief that it's relationships, not features and functions that sell products. Yes, they need to have a decent product to sell, but beyond that, it's the relationships that count.

It's easy to disdain this point of view, but it's an important dimension to understand if you want to steer around political potholes.

COMMUNICATION

"Good communication" does not equal providing a robust status report. These reports almost always contain information that means a lot to the IT professionals working on the project – like the features built into the system and the milestones reached – but has little value to the business clients. Business clients want to know what these accomplishments mean for them and how they contribute to their own goals, as well as what they can expect from IT in the future.

IT professionals need to stop talking about the features and functions of the project and talk more about the business outcomes, and they have to do this outside of written reports. The best communication is achieved face-to-face – you can't build a relationship via email.

FOCUS

When leading or managing a project, IT professionals need to define the goals of the project and intently focus on these goals. And this doesn't mean being "on time, on budget and according to spec." They need to dig deeper than that and define the desired business outcomes of the project and then translate those goals into what they as IT professionals need to achieve. It might be a change in behavior among a particular client base or the establishment and acceptance of a new process. This is furthered discussed in Chapter 7 on gathering business requirements.

Focusing on these goals will help reveal your natural allies, as well as the clients who may feel threatened by the project's implications.

INTERESTS

What's every business clients' favorite radio station? WIIFM. By tuning your antenna to that frequency, you're in a much better position to understand the motivation behind people's actions, as well as figure out strategies for encouraging them in the direction you want them to move.

Henry Ford once said, "There is one principle which a man must follow if he wishes to succeed, and that is to understand human nature. I am convinced by my own experience, and by that of others, that if there is any secret of success, it lies in the ability to get another's point of view and see things from his angle as well as from your own."

FLEXIBILITY

The business world is not a place of black-and-white, right-or-wrong decisions. What's more, IT can't claim ownership of "the right answer," because what might appear to be the right answer from a technology point of view is not always the right answer for the business.

I once worked with an IT organization that identified two different technology solutions for a particular business situation. Solution A had the lowest maintenance costs and was a good fit with the existing IT infrastructure. Solution B required twice as much work for IT, in terms of supporting additional technologies and needing to hire more people. The organization presented Solution A as the "best" alternative.

But look more carefully at this logic – all the reasons for selecting A over B were internally focused and geared toward the convenience of IT. The IT organization was oblivious to the fact that Solution B might result in three times as much benefit to the business.

It's easy for people to develop tunnel vision about things that they think are important, but success requires adjusting your own point of view. Instead of laying out what you think is a logical argument and expecting everyone to get on board, you need to consider that your preference is not always "the right answer." A better approach is presenting all the alternatives with the information required to make the best decision – not presenting the most convenient decision for IT.

TRUST

Effective alliances can't be forged unless people trust you. What erodes trust is when IT comes across has having its own agenda rather than striving to understand the client's point of view.

If you don't think trust is important, consider this classic scenario. A project is under way, with IT developing a solution for a client. The project gets derailed, however, because a vendor meets the client at a golf tournament, begins interacting with the client directly – going around the project manager – and steers the client to the vendor's point of view. What happened there? The vendor understood the importance of gaining the client's trust. Instead of wondering why this type of scenario can happen, you can learn from it and begin building your own trusting relationships.

SUPPORT

A great way to strengthen relationships is to figure out ways you can be helpful to people, outside the current project's parameters. What keeps your clients awake at night, or what do they dwell on in the shower? If you ever need a favor from someone, it's easier to ask if you've previously helped him or her out.

Here again, listening is key. Let's say you're having a meeting with a client who has just gotten off the phone and appears distracted. "Sorry," he says, "I'm just really irritated – let's get on with our meeting." What if you encouraged him to tell you what's going on? You might find out he's been back-and-forth with his wife all day over a dispute with their DSL provider. Take it a step further – can you offer to get him in touch with someone you know in telecom that has contacts with the company?

With one simple phone call, you might be able to build a lot of trust and influence with this client that will reap benefits in the future. It has nothing to do with the project, but indirectly, this type of encounter is just as important as meeting a project deadline.

CONFLICT MANAGEMENT

Things go wrong – it's a truth of any project. That's why it's so important to improve our ability to handle these conflicts and learn to negotiate effectively.

Negotiating means figuring out a way for everyone to feel they've won something. And that means you can't draw a line in the sand – the "I'm right, you're wrong" mentality. By putting yourself in the other person's shoes, you can better work toward your real goal: Getting people from where they are to where you want them to be. And that means figuring out how far you're willing to move to get to that win-win position. Negotiating through conflict is so important that we've dedicated Chapter 5 to that topic.

For instance, a newly hired graphics designer approaches IT and asks for a new PC. IT gives him three options, all IBM PC-compatibles. Of course, the designer was thinking more along the lines of a Macintosh – the standard in the graphics design industry but definitely outside the parameters of IT's established architecture. This can turn into a standoff, where IT imposes its will on the graphics designer. Of course, the graphics department will likely sneak out and buy what they need from someone else.

A better option would be for IT to allow well-considered exceptions to their architecture. If the graphics department commits to paying for the extra cost of maintaining a Macintosh, IT can permit the variance. Both parties get what they need to be successful. It's when IT draws its lines so deeply that it can't see win-win opportunities, which means they become ineffective conflict managers.

CONCLUSION

IT can no longer play the role of bystander in the game of corporate politics. Technology projects today mean change to the status quo, especially as companies use technology to break down traditional silos that exist across their ever-growing and increasingly global businesses. It bears repeating: Where there's technology, there's change, and where there's change, there will be people who perceive themselves as winners and as losers. And that's where political behaviors are born.

It's true that few IT professionals go into this field with the desire to "play politics." But you don't have to become a negative and devious politician; you just need to develop the political savvy to positively influence or even overcome the inevitable politics that technology projects create.

In fact, ignoring the inflammatory nature of IT's work as a change instigator is a perilous practice. Having been awakened to its importance for project success, there is no reason that IT professionals can't learn to navigate the sea of corporate politics.

Tactics for Sharpening Your Political Savvy

10. If you're not influencing your client base, someone else is.

9. It's relationships that sell, not the product itself.

8. Even people way down on the organizational chart can be strong allies – or enemies.

7. Relationships don't exist without trust.

6. The business world isn't always fair – learn enough to predict actions others may take.

5. Don't be a victim or a sideline-sitter.

4. Enlarge your radar to understand the world outside of IT.

3. Water cooler conversations aren't just a waste of time – they can reveal important hidden truths.

2. It's a lot easier to ask someone for a favor when you've helped them with something previously.

1. Conflict management means figuring out a way for everyone to win.

SPECIFIC ACTIONS I WILL TAKE

✔

✔

✔

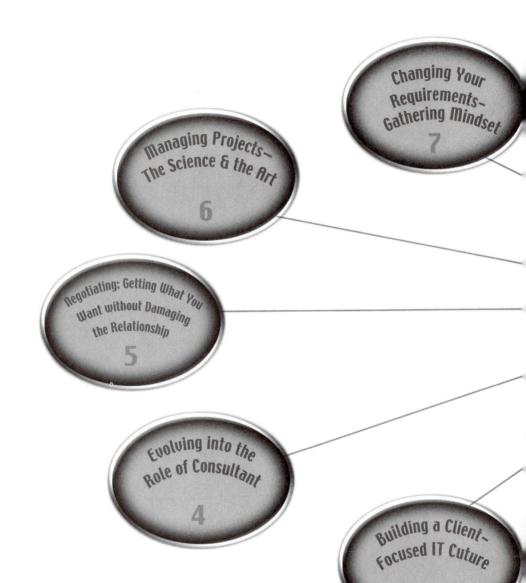

Changing Your
Requirements–
Gathering Mindset

7

Managing Projects–
The Science & the Art

6

Negotiating: Getting What You
Want without Damaging
the Relationship

5

Evolving into the
Role of Consultant

4

Building a Client–
Focused IT Cuture

3

Sharpening Your
Political Savvy
8

Driving Change
with Intent
10

Marketing
IT's Value
9

Creating Your 21st
Century Workforce
and Culture
1

Transforming Your
IT Team
2

now that you've read this far into the book and have begun to apply the strategies and philosophies my colleagues espouse, you're ready to tackle marketing. We've purposefully put this chapter at the end of the book, because no one can start marketing their IT organization until they've developed their staff's leadership capabilities and helped it adopt a service-oriented and consultative mindset, with well-honed skills in project management, political savvy, business requirements gathering and negotiating.

In fact, I believe marketing is the most important of the business disciplines and can be the most fun, as you'll soon discover. The formulation of the IT organization's image as "service provider of choice" is one of the most important factors for a successful IT cultural transformation. By and large our clients don't understand what we do. We need to market internally to have a shot at increasing our credibility, building partnerships and turning around any negative perceptions. We live in a world where perception matters, and this is particularly true for internal IT organizations in today's business world. Let's face it – for the most part, our clients don't understand what IT does. If they perceive us as mere code changers, network fixers and PC installers, how will they react when IT tries to move into a more strategic role in the organization?

In other cases, IT damages its own image and reputation by projecting an arrogant air that says, "We know what's best for the business because we're the technical experts." This looks even worse when the organization hasn't taken the time to explain how technology can be a strategic advantage to the business. Meanwhile, IT is competing with external outsourcers, consultants, vendors and system integrators, all of which are very adept at getting in front of executive-level decision makers to convince them of the business benefits their companies can provide.

All these reasons explain why IT needs to market internally – to have a shot at increasing its credibility, building partnerships and turning around any negative perceptions.

And that's where marketing comes in. It's not about hype and empty promises; it's about creating an awareness of IT's value. It's about changing client perceptions by presenting a clear, consistent message about the value of IT. After all, if you don't market yourself, someone else will, and you might not like the image you end up with.

At this point, you might be asking yourself, "How do I begin to market? My IT staff doesn't even like the 'M' word!" Well, you're not alone.

Remember the television ad of the software salesman standing outside the busy executive's door, hounding him with the repeating slogan of, "Soooo, how much software do you wanna buy?" That's what most IT staffers think when they hear the word, "marketing." They wonder, "What does marketing have to do with IT? Why do I need to change my image? I'm already a good developer!" Because marketing is simply not their comfort zone, they revert to what is more natural for them, which is doing their technical job and leaving the job of marketing to someone else, reinforcing the image of, "IT is just a bunch of techies." As you will soon see, it is everybody's job to market if you want to obtain the full benefits of your marketing efforts.

Yet many IT organizations have done a very poor job of marketing their capabilities. Even marketing-savvy IT leaders struggle with how to effectively encourage their staffs to adopt a marketing philosophy and consistently promote their ability to be IT supplier of choice within their organizations.

But I've seen IT organizations that – through formal and informal marketing techniques – are now enjoying increased staff productivity, improved customer loyalty and a widely held belief in IT's value, not to mention increased project awareness, momentum and buy-in. When IT staffs develop credibility and then reinforce that image through their day-to-day interactions with clients, they'll find themselves invited to the table when C-level executives gather to discuss strategic opportunities and initiatives.

In fact, during my 25 years in the IT profession and working with clients throughout the U.S. and internationally, I've seen IT leaders make great strides in recognizing the strategic advantage of marketing the IT organization to the rest of the company. One client I worked with put together a marketing initiative to key executives that resulted in more business. "More business?" you say; "Why do I need more work to do?" Well, the executives at this particular CIO's company were getting ready to outsource the work to an outside consulting firm. That would have created a whole new set of headaches for the IT department, so the CIO was thrilled that they could keep this in-house.

Another client in the banking industry put together an initiative called "The Key Influencer Program." This IT organization was proactive in researching how it could apply technology to help its company gain a competitive edge in the marketplace and reported their findings to the top brass every six months in a roundtable format. This went a long way in helping to build a positive perception of the IT department.

So, the first step is marketing to the IT organization that marketing is a good thing. This can be done a number of ways, but the most effective is to let your IT staff know how important this is to your success and help them feel accountable for marketing. To elicit positive marketing behaviors from the entire IT team, IT leaders need to tie the marketing mindset to measurements that provide incentive and reward.

I learned about the importance of marketing soon after embarking on my IT career. I had just finished college and was all set to program in Fortran IV. I also knew just enough about marketing to make me dangerous. I was fortunate to land a job with a Fortune 100 computer manufacturing company in Silicon Valley and started doing technical support instead of programming. One of my responsibilities was conducting presentations about our hardware line to potential buyers. Through trial and error, I discovered I would get a lot more applause at the end of my speech if I spiced it up with a little more pizzazz, a lot more benefit statements (WIIFMs) and a bit less on features and functions (this is the critical concept of "What's In It For Me?" defined in the introduction to this book). So I started looking for WIIFMs every chance I got, and it became second nature to rattle them off. I guess this got the attention of the vice president, because the next thing I knew, I was plucked from my comfort zone and put in charge of marketing a portfolio of products and services for the IT department to offer our clients. Back to school I went, to bone up on marketing strategies and advertising campaigns. Because at the end of the day, I still wanted that applause.

Over the years, marketing has served me well in all the other parts of my career – in management, consulting and training. And through my many years working with IT organizations on their marketing initiatives, I've developed a six-step approach to marketing the value of IT.

STEP 1

Marketing to the IT Department

The best way to begin your marketing efforts is to embed a 24×7 marketing mindset throughout the entire organization, not just in one or two people. Whether our staffs know it or not, marketing has become part of their everyday jobs. Every time they speak with a client or attend a meeting, they create a positive or negative perception in the client's mind for the new system they're implementing, the processes they use to get something done, the organization they work for and whether they're capable of adding business value or can barely be trusted to keep the e-mail system running.

So the idea of 24×7 marketing is a key mindset we need to develop in our staffs. They need to become what O&A calls "hallway marketers," which means they should s peak positively about IT every opportunity they get – in the hallway, elevator, parking lot, cafeteria, during and after meetings and even during social outings.

Even simple changes in phrasing can make a world of difference in how staff members project an image of themselves, their attitude toward their work and their willingness to help their clients. If a client asks when an application is likely to get delivered, for instance, a typical IT professional might say, "We can't deliver that until next Tuesday." Think of how different an impression would be made if they instead responded, "We can deliver that application as early as next Tuesday." Or if a client reports a problem with a recent system upgrade, some IT professionals might say, "I'm not sure where we messed up on that." Wouldn't it be better if they were to say, "We'll look into that and call you by the end of the day."

One client in Canada went as far as publishing a 3×5 mini brochure for the IT department called "Business Value Delivered: The IT Professional's Guide to Delivering Value." Along with the printed vision statement, it also contains the foundation principles of service, change management and leadership qualities expected of the IT department. Sprinkled throughout are pictures of the IT professionals helping clients.

Another idea is to develop a tag line that creates an identity with which all IT staffers can relate. This will also spill over to your client base as they begin to see a "brand recognition" that they can identify with. One client in Northern California took its tag line one-step further and created logos on company-colored polo shirts. Over the pocket was an oval with the tag line, "Tech IT Easy." The message was, "We want to make it easy to do business with us." It was a step towards turning around the perception of the department.

At this point, I might add that it will behoove you to include your technical staff in creating these types of creative endeavors. It not only increases their level of buy-in to your marketing efforts, but it can also be fun and a good team-building exercise. You might even be surprised at how creative the analytical thinkers can be. At one point in my career as an IT manager, I had the opportunity to run an Executive Briefing Center for the many customers who bought our company's computers. Our IT area was responsible for assisting the sales people in the technical explanations of our fine hardware. The presentations were held in a beautiful mahogany and marble suite on the ninth floor overlooking Interstate 101.

This new center needed some spiffy color glossy brochures and some brand recognition. After all, we were competing for the time and attention of many busy CEOs, with all the other technology centers deep in the heart of Silicon Valley. Thus, we embarked on a brand-recognition campaign.

The corporate office had already named our center, "The Application Center for Technology," so there wasn't much we could do about changing the name. So a group of us "technologists" huddled together in a conference room hashing out various ideas for a tag line. We settled on, "The **S**an **J**ose **A**pplication **C**enter for **T**echnology ... a great ACT to follow." We were not only more creative than we ever thought we could be, but the whole team also felt an affinity for our new home. And we took it a step further with a silver lightning bolt symbol across the front cover of all collateral materials to signify the new networking connections of TCP/IP over Ethernet (OK, that was a long time ago!).

If it helps your staff, you can think of marketing as "educating" the clients. One CIO I worked with knew that the word "marketing" wouldn't go over so well, so he substituted the words "Marketing Plan" with "Quality Improvement Plan" (QIP). In essence, he was marketing to the IT staff in terms they could relate to.

This astute CIO also knew that if he handled the rollout of the QIP correctly, he would weed out tedious, low-value tasks and gain more time for satisfying strategic planning work. This was a benefit he stated to the troops during his Quality Town Hall Meeting, to gain their buy-in.

STEP 2

Build Partnerships

Establishing working relationships with clients can be difficult because it's outside of many IT professionals' comfort zone. But better working relationships build trust and credibility. And trust and credibility are directly tied to people's motivation to work collaboratively. These elements must be in place before we can market our services, and my colleagues, in earlier chapters of the book, have already established the importance of client partnerships.

Both casual and formal interactions can show clients that IT is interested in them and in their needs. For informal interactions, it's absolutely essential to learn how to actively listen to clients, which means acknowledging their issues, listening and responding with empathy and taking ownership to help them. Active listening is so important that we cover it in-depth in our chapter on consulting skills.

Another way that IT leaders can help prepare their IT staffs to take advantage of informal client encounters is to develop and distribute positive "press statements" or "party lines" for all new projects, upgrades, rollouts and implementations that went smoothly, as well as those that didn't go so smoothly. With these tools, the staff can easily draw upon the type of wording that will best establish the new perception you're trying to create. These press statements should be clear, concise and client-focused, not long, elaborate PowerPoint presentations. Remember that marketing is a 24×7 mindset, and you will want to do "hallway marketing" at every casual client encounter.

There are also more formal ways to strengthen client relationships, like planning visits to their workplace. At one large manufacturer, the IT leader encourages members of his team to schedule regular visits to the company's 18 plants to make sure that all systems are functioning smoothly and to ward off potential problems. The staff spends time talking to customers to ferret out any issues – even if they haven't called the help desk to fix them.

Another director of IT that I worked with established the "MBWA Program." Using Tom Peters' "Management By Walking Around" concept, he conducts scheduled and unscheduled visits to his clients on a routine basis to get to know them better and build relationships. At one such visit, the client went to retrieve some information off the mainframe, and the IT director watched in horror as it took 30 seconds to fill the screen. His client casually mentioned that this was typical. With one phone call, the IT director was able to get a much better response time for his client. He told me, "I would never have known about this issue if I hadn't been doing a little MBWA."

STEP 3

Differentiate Yourself

To differentiate the IT organization effectively, you first must understand what matters most to your client. Clients have different business drivers and different intrinsic motivators – in other words, different reasons for making the decisions they make.

For example, take a look at automobile advertisements on television. Have you ever noticed that different ads appeal to different motivations or market segments? If you watch an ad for a Cadillac, you'll notice they're appealing to the status and image mindset of the buyer. For Volvo, the campaign is around safety and security. For Saturn, the value being emphasized is economy and getting the best bang for your buck. These advertisements are soliciting to the core values, or intrinsic motivators, of the consumer. The same concept applies to marketing in IT. You will want to appeal to the core values or intrinsic motivators of your client, as well as the business motivators of your client. Business motivators, or benefits, include things like increasing market share, decreasing costs, improving efficiencies and increasing profits.

I often see IT leaders make the mistake of enthusiastically embarking on a marketing effort that focuses on all the great technology the organization has implemented or plans to implement. Even IT organizations that have made great strides as marketers still talk too much about the features of their systems and services without focusing on how those features benefit clients and the business.

Making technology your marketing focus is like trying to climb a ladder without stepping on all the rungs. You're reaching too far, too soon, and by skipping all those steps in between, you're putting yourself in an unnecessarily precarious situation, with no guarantee you'll make it all the way to the top.

For instance, say you've implemented a new firewall or just completed a system upgrade. You can't expect clients to get all excited about new security features or faster speeds and feeds. They want to know what the business benefit is. How does the firewall improve their work lives? Does the upgrade mean reports will get into their hands faster? How can they make better business decisions because IT has implemented the next version of software? The answers to these questions must be clearly articulated by IT, and yet much of the time, we don't do that.

It's the difference between looking through a pure technology lens and trying to see things from the perspective of the client. I was working with a client in Oregon who told me the following story: She was visiting a client to determine business requirements when the client said to her, "You IT people are like used car salesmen. All you talk about is technology."

She said she learned a valuable lesson that day – always speak in terms the client understands.

That's why IT leaders need to learn how to package their organization's day-to-day communications, business cases and marketing plans in terms of business outcomes and client WIIFMs. We need to focus our efforts on promoting the business problem-solving capabilities of IT. Remember the old sales adage, "People don't buy drill bits because they want a drill bit. People buy drill bits because they want a hole."

STEP 4

Establish Credibility

Peter F. Drucker argued, "Business has only two functions – marketing and innovation." I propose a corollary that in marketing, "presentation and perception are everything."

We already discussed the importance of hallway marketing and creating a positive impression of the IT department 24×7. But it's not easy to know how others perceive us. We think we're smart, witty and reasonable, while others perceive us as sarcastic, self-serving and helplessly removed from reality. One way to be sure you know how IT is perceived is to conduct a survey. A simple questionnaire with easy Yes/No check boxes will give you the information you need. Ask your clients to rate your staff on some of the following:

- Are we professional and courteous?

- Do we provide quick response time?

- Do we understand your business needs?

- Do we provide alternatives to problems?

What you want to do is assess the level of trust your clients have in you and your team, and uncover any expectations you weren't aware of so you can address any problems with a concrete marketing plan.

I saw this most successfully achieved when I was in a consulting role for O&A back in 1999. One of the most successful CIOs I know, and also one of my favorites for creative thinking outside the box, hired O&A to conduct a survey of key agency heads in the county in which he was employed. He had heard some rumblings that the IT department wasn't perceived as positively as it could have been. In fact, since he was recently hired by the county as the new CIO, there was even more skepticism about what changes he might invoke. Obviously, there was a lot of mistrust between IT and the client base.

As a result of the survey, a marketing plan was put in place to address each agency director's key concerns about the IT department. This CIO literally went about changing the perception one by one through a formal plan. Fast-forward five years, and I'll tell you that this CIO was able to go from a rating of "No Trust" from most agencies to being honored as one of the top 100 CIOs in the country by *Computerworld* magazine. Ironically enough, it was one of the toughest agency directors that nominated him for this prestigious award.

STEP 5

Create Product/Service Awareness

Now that you've built strong relationships, increased your credibility through positive press statements and hallway marketing, demonstrated that you understand client needs and WIIFMs, you are finally ready to market your products and services.

In my work with clients, I often hear, "I'm not sure what IT even does." And worse yet, I hear from IT employees, "I don't even know what other IT departments do." So before you can market the added value you bring to the business, you must let business clients – and each other – know what you already offer.

To do this, some IT organizations stage open houses, inviting directors and managers and other key staff to educate them on the services that IT provides and on how to better communicate their technology needs and issues. They might reinforce the message with pamphlets documenting IT's services and key phone numbers, as well as brochures giving customers tips on how to solve some of the most common IT-related problems.

One client I worked with was about to move the call center from one location to a brand-new building. The IT organization took this opportunity to market the event as a "Grand Re-Opening" with a new tag line, new furniture and a new catchy help desk phone number of IT-911. It sent out invitations to directors and managers in the businesses and asked them to bring key staff. A tour of the new facility followed a brief presentation on how the new call center would operate. The organization also handed out a pamphlet, documenting its services and how best to get in touch with the help desk, as well as a brochure providing tips on the Top 10 Frequently Asked Questions at the Help Desk. Refreshments were served, and trinkets were handed out with the call center's name and new phone number on them.

Another IT organization held a weeklong "IT Spirit Week" in its headquarters, presenting demos and tutorials, as well as a simple lunch for clients who stopped by to learn more about IT and its services. The week culminated with an ice cream social and a drawing for a few flat-screen monitors.

One of my favorites is the client who revamped the "Brown Bag Lunchtime Seminar" as "The Gold Bag Executive Luncheon." Once a quarter, this IT department hosts a catered lunch for their C-level executives in the dining room. They give a presentation on the latest and greatest technology that the execs have been reading about in in-flight airline magazines and discuss how this technology may or may not fit the corporate architecture. It sounds like it's a bit on the techy side, but it actually helps the executives get a handle on what's possible in their company from a strategic advantage perspective.

In another case, I know a savvy IT director in Los Angeles who planned a way to showcase her new team after a recent merger between two companies and subsequently two IT departments. She invited Midwest clients who weren't familiar with the new IT department to a tour of the data center, followed by tickets to a Dodgers game. It was a big hit and helped build morale during the merger and forge new relationships, at the same time introducing the new IT department.

Lastly, I'd like to tell the story about one of the first pieces of marketing collateral I ever created. It was a quick guide to the services our IT organization offered outside our company. Our client base was the sales organization that would be selling our technical services to our outside customers. We came up with what we thought was a pretty catchy guidebook, with a working title of, "Selling IT Services." Before we put it into print, however, we brought it to several client focus groups that told us it was boring and not compelling enough. After much deliberation, we revamped it to, "The EASY Way to Sell IT Services," and it was a big hit.

This leads me to an important part of marketing, and that is the use of what I like to call "magic words." Magic words are special words that capture the attention of customers, like "easy," "new," "announcing," "free" and "how to." However, it's important to note that not only must your collateral fit the needs of the client, but it also must avoid being too glitzy if IT is perceived as a high-overhead organization. Think it through – are color handouts necessary when black-and-white will do? If you're too professional looking in your marketing materials, you may fall prey to criticism of over-spending on marketing.

STEP 6

Develop a Formal Plan

You might be thinking that the last thing IT needs is yet another plan. But savvy IT leaders ensure that marketing plans are developed and executed at multiple levels of the organization, such as the executive level, business unit level and team level.

Just like any project plan, there are many factors to consider when rolling out a marketing plan. A few of these include:

- The overall goal of the marketing plan – what you hope to accomplish with it and ways to evaluate its success. For example, do you want to market your image and credibility or go right to marketing value-add? How will you know you've been successful?

- Risks and assumptions, as well as factors to consider that might hinder the marketing effort, such as corporate culture and reorganization timing.

- Types of awareness programs and relationship-building strategies you can realistically roll out, given budget and staff restrictions.

- Tag lines and themes to garner brand recognition.

- Factors that might impact successful marketing, such as past history or perceptions by the clients.

After reviewing these considerations, put your conclusions in writing so that you have a well-thought-out marketing strategy or even a checklist that the entire team can get behind. Anticipate any questions or reactions you might get and have a response plan. Here's where your press statements come in.

DETERMINING SUCCESS

So, how do you know when you've succeeded with your marketing efforts? What are the indicators of a good marketing plan? Number one is defining upfront what will determine success, not waiting until the end. You need to know before you begin what you want to happen as a result of your efforts.

Other indicators include:

- Your clients requesting that IT be more involved in their business, such as inviting you to business planning and strategy meetings or having you review and influence their technology decisions.

- Having your budget requests met without having to constantly justify your existence and contributions.

- Your current clients referring others to you, or that you can imagine your clients saying, "Hey, IT really helped us out," vs. "Oh, those IT people!"

- Requests for your assistance becoming more focused and more in line with the products and services you actually provide.

- Unsolicited positive feedback both formal and informal from your clients and senior management.

- Morale across IT is high.

- IT being included in merger and acquisition negotiations and due diligence.

- IT being included in meetings and sales processes with big C-level clients.

A word to the wise: There's no guarantee that everyone will automatically applaud the services you're marketing. After all, clients have a past history with IT and perhaps some preconceived notions of what IT people are all about. To be successful in executing your marketing efforts, you need to anticipate and plan for the factors that can derail them. Solid marketing plans acknowledge and address both positive and negative impacts upfront, with an appropriate press statement to minimize resistance.

For example, imagine you were marketing your new mission statement. What about the client group that's constantly asking you to provide wireless services, which is not part of your mission? You can anticipate that they'll be less than thrilled with your message, unless you plan a response to any questions they have about their wireless needs.

Take into consideration other negative impact factors, such as:

- Past history or perceptions that clients have had with the marketing effort.

- External or internal competition.

- Economic factors such as budgets.

- Corporate culture factors such as politics or impending reorganizations.

- Current projects or systems that aren't being well received.

- Technical constraints, such as standards, security and documentation.

CONCLUSION

For many IT professionals, it requires a dramatic change of mindset to start promoting the work they do. But it's worth it, because it's becoming a crucial element of the IT leader's job to show the business that the IT organization is capable of being the strategic business partner of choice.

We can begin by understanding how our organizations are perceived– rightly or wrongly – and then crafting a plan for gaining control over how we want to be understood. This can be accomplished by bridging gaps of miscommunication with clients; understanding their needs and strategic objectives and then showing them the IT organization is capable of meeting those needs. When business clients develop a new awareness of IT's true value, the IT organization's own marketing message can be heard above the very aggressive campaigns launched by internal IT's competitors – external vendors and service providers.

When you combine a marketing mindset focusing on the client, and add in some positive hallway marketing, you'll get a successful, well positioned, marketing-savvy IT organization whose value is understood enterprise-wide.

Approaches for Marketing IT's Value

10. Conduct internal market research to better understand client needs.

9. Develop a mission statement, clear goals and objectives that define who you are.

8. Design a tag line that the whole team can endorse.

7. Create a promotional strategy that is long-term and high-impact.

6. Develop long-term client relationships.

5. Design positive press statements for use in hallway marketing.

4. Forge stronger partnerships with your most difficult clients.

3. Adopt a frame of mind that constantly asks "Who is my client?" and "What services can I offer that client?"

2. Project a team image by changing "I" to "We."

1. Speak in terms of benefits rather than features.

SPECIFIC ACTIONS I WILL TAKE

✔

✔

✔

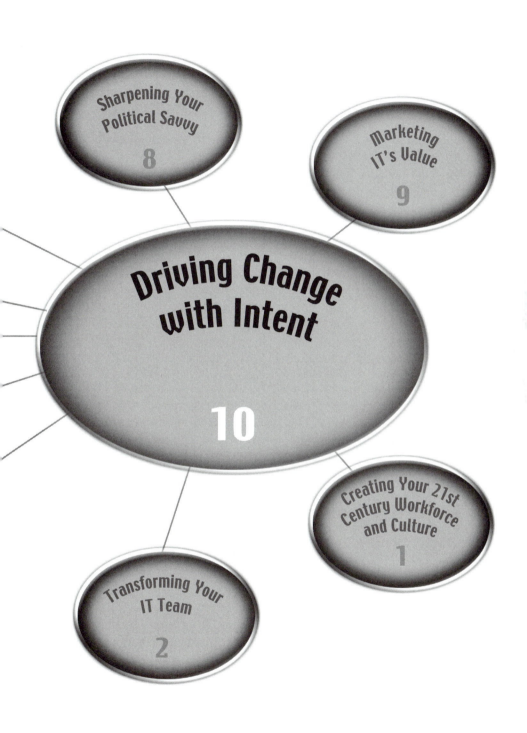

The topic of change has been a constant theme throughout this book. Whether you are leading large scale organizational transformation initiatives, a large or small project, or expanding the skills and capabilities of your workforce, you are embarking upon change. And that is precisely why we saved this chapter for the end.

Today's business world is one of change – constant, inevitable, unending change. And in this world, the *only* people who will survive are those who learn to turn on a dime. It's true for companies, as well – those who effectively create a culture of change are the ones rising to the top of the marketplace.

Nowhere is this more true than within the IT organization. Not only do IT leaders need to embrace change, but in many cases, they're also the ones shouldered with the responsibility of making change happen throughout the enterprise. Look at what IT does every day – whether it's helping the company develop more innovative products or services, hone the bottom line, streamline the supply chain or comply with new regulations, the projects that IT is involved in always involve aspects of change – to people, processes, systems or all three.

You might wonder then, why IT leaders don't spend time focused on the possibility of these types of changes not taking place, especially considering the risks involved – the risk of delays or running over budget, the risk that the new tool or system doesn't get used as planned or doesn't meet the business objective. The fact is, change doesn't "just happen." Like an event or project, successful change has to be planned, structured, monitored and led, with purpose and intent. But that's not how change is usually treated.

From what we've seen in our years of working with IT, most CIOs and other IT leaders are very aware of change. But they simply don't have the know-how to manage it through to successful completion. They might put a risk mitigation strategy in place, involving plans to address the more obvious risks, and they might do some contingency planning and preparation. But only rarely do we see an IT organization apply the same amount of rigor toward planning for and driving the components of change necessary for success.

We've all seen what happens when change goes unmanaged. The targeted users of the system never really commit to the project or embrace their new responsibilities. People become disengaged and even hostile, refusing to get involved with any stage of the project or even sabotaging the effort. Excuses are given: "Well if they would just go to training," or, "We delivered exactly what they asked for on time and on budget; I don't know why they aren't seeing the results stated in their business case."

In some cases, we've heard IT leaders complain that even though they've sent out e-mails and memos regarding a big initiative and all the changes it entails, people still don't seem to get it. "I've communicated about this for six months," they say, "and people say they never heard about it!" It's no wonder most organizations believe their organizational transformation efforts and change initiatives are only marginally successful at best.

It's up to IT to play this role, to help the people affected by the system understand, accept and ultimately embrace the changes wrought by the initiative. And the leaders and organizations that aren't doing this – and developing the skills and tools to make change happen – will simply be seen as ineffective, costly and, ultimately, replaceable.

In this chapter, we hope to pass along some of what we've learned about what change leadership and a culture of change can look like. Anyone can do it, as long as they know about the dynamics of change and learn the structures, tools and skills to lead and manage it.

Defining Terms

Throughout this chapter, we use terminology that's a bit different from other chapters in the book. For instance, we use the term, "target users" to refer to anyone impacted by the change, at any level, whether it's a change to their business process, the technology they use, the way they behave or the nature of their relationships.

There are also three essential roles that need to be filled, both by IT staff and by others in the business community. It's up to the IT group to identify the right people to play these roles. The three roles include change leader, change agent and change advocate. Change leaders are the people who sponsor and validate the project that's causing the change to occur. There are usually a number of individuals assigned to this role, and it's important that they be placed broadly and deeply throughout the organization.

The second – change agents are the people who plan, facilitate and implement key change activities. And the last – change advocates (also called "opinion leaders") are the people required to achieve successful change. We'll get into these roles more specifically later in the chapter.

THE COMPONENTS OF CHANGE

To start down the path of becoming an effective leader of change, it's important to understand the components of change – commitment, community and clarity – as well as the "glue" that brings them all together: communication.

We've put together a simple model (below) to help you understand these components and how they interact. Notice first that change is represented with a triangle and three conjoined circles, not with squares connected by arrows. We've done this purposefully because the components are all inter-related, and they're also not linear. While there are checklists within each component, it's not like a flowchart, where you close the book on one task and then move onto the next. Change is not linear; it's a dynamic process. Let's move through these components, starting with commitment.

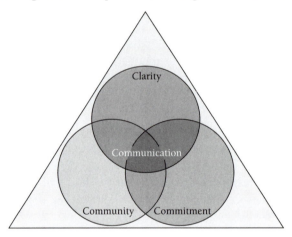

SECTION 1

Achieving Commitment Is Essential for Sustaining Change

When thinking about change it is important to understand the difference between compliance and commitment. Compliance means going along with a recommendation or new process without really believing in it. It's when you're mandated into changing your behavior without changing your mindset. And it means it wouldn't take much to knock you off course or make you go back to your old ways when no one is looking.

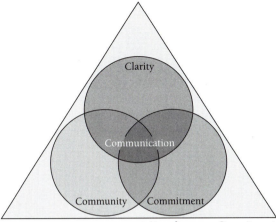

- Compliance vs. Commitment
- Changing Minds
- Understanding resistance
- Emotional Cycle of Change

Commitment means being bound emotionally and intellectually to a course of action or to another person. It leads to sustained behavioral change. Commitment is very personal – no one can "make" another person commit to something; people have to make that jump themselves. And when they do, they're full participants – they believe in what they're doing and where they're heading, and they're intent on completing the journey.

We've heard some people say, "You don't need commitment at work," or, "If commitment requires my 'soul,' I won't give my soul to my job," or, "All you need is a commitment for compliance." These are nice catchphrases, and maybe you agree with one or all of them, but we certainly don't. If the definition of commitment involves buy-in, then you've got to align your mind, body and soul to the effort.

Most of the time, without even thinking about it, IT leaders get compliance rather than commitment from target users. And then they wonder why, six months later, people aren't embracing the new process or system they delivered. It's because they weren't truly committed! The fact is, failing to achieve commitment is the single most important reason why IT organizations cannot sustain change.

It's true that gaining commitment from others is a difficult challenge, primarily because you can't change another person's mind; they have to do it for themselves. An individual's mindset involves his or her internal beliefs, philosophies and values. This is classified information and difficult to assess. But while achieving true commitment can be challenging, the payoff is huge. Imagine if every team member and user of the new system completely bought into the new features, functions, tools and processes. Think about how easy training would be, how great it would be that instead of people complaining about the change, they're providing feedback on continuous improvement. They're tolerating the bumps in the road because they believe the end goal is worth the wait. Isn't this worth your time and energy? Focus on achieving the commitment level required for your project to succeed.

There are times that full commitment isn't necessary. In some cases – say a new time tracking system – the target user might grumpily comply with a new process because doing otherwise would be personally detrimental; in this example, he or she wouldn't get paid. But many initiatives bear high risk for the company, not the target user directly, and failure to get them in place could turn into costly debacles, impacting the top and bottom lines. To know which you need – commitment or compliance – just ask yourself what's the risk if target users don't get on-board?

In other cases, there's simply not time to go for full commitment at the beginning of the project. But that doesn't mean you should stop trying to attain it and give up. In these cases, it's important to work purposefully toward the goal of commitment over time to secure it.

When working toward commitment, it's important to remember that resistance is a natural part of change. Depending on the severity as perceived by the individual, it's as if their survival instinct kicks in, and the feeling of loss can be overwhelming. People's natural inclination is to protect themselves, preserve their competence, maintain their comfort zone or stay in line with their personal values. Everyone has an individual capacity for change, and when they reach their limit, they can become frustrated and overwhelmed, with potentially diminished returns.

Most IT leaders just ignore resistance, or worse, say things like, "Just get with the program," driving people further into resistance or, at best, compliance. As an effective leader of change, you should expect resistance. You should never be surprised when it occurs. In fact, we challenge you to go so far as to anticipate it. Set up a safe environment to explore it. Resistance brings new information and tells you that the individual has energy invested. Your job, as a leader of change, is to turn their energy from a negative state to a positive one. In doing so, you allow for an opportunity to build commitment.

To better understand resistance and other natural responses to change, we talk about the psychology of change during our Leading Change workshop. Studies have shown that people who are responding to unwanted or unwelcome change tend to move through what we call "the emotional cycles of change," which are similar to the Kübler-Ross model of the "five stages of grief" – denial, anger, bargaining, depression and acceptance.

In order to lead people through change, it's important to identify where target users are in the cycle and know how to help them move into the acceptance stage as quickly as possible. Following are the emotional cycles of change and a brief word on how to handle them:

Immobilization. This is brought on by anxiety, fear and confusion. The best approach is to accept and acknowledge these emotions, while repeatedly offering brief, clear information and support.

Denial. At this stage, people are unable to accurately absorb information or participate appropriately. The best approach is to continue providing information and team them up with someone who's moved to the acceptance phase.

Anger. Don't take this phase personally. Allow target users to vent these emotions, while listening carefully for issues that are real and need to be addressed.

Bargaining. At this stage, it's important to help individuals get involved in the changes and feel a part of the action. You can listen to people's suggestions, being careful to consider which ones actually fit, while dismissing those that don't. You can start setting specific tasks with specific timeframes and establish consequences of noncompliance.

Depression. People in this stage need support and empathy, as well as encouragement to take responsibility. You can break tasks into small segments and reinforce success, while talking to individuals and setting up forums where they can air their concerns and provide input.

Testing. Individuals in this stage begin to get involved with the changes happening around them. It's important to establish clear boundaries and parameters while helping people explore realistic options.

Acceptance. People are seeing the potentials within the change and are adjusting or adapting to it. People's efforts need to be recognized, and progress should be acknowledged.

Section 2

Change Takes a Community

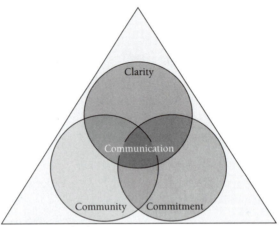

- ◆ Changing Leadership
- ◆ Key Roles in the Change Process
- ◆ Transition Structures
- ◆ Network of Resources

The second component of change is Community, because driving change is more akin to a symphony orchestra than a soloist. In other words, it takes different people collaborating together in diverse roles to make it work. It's up to IT leaders to identify and engage the right people to play the carefully scripted roles mentioned earlier in the chapter, including that of change leader, change advocate and change agent.

We call this community of people the "transition structure." Some companies formalize these three roles by creating a change management office. For instance, one global retailer that embarked on a $650 million project over a six-year timeframe created a three-person change management office as part of its transition structure. But the important thing is not how you structure these roles but that you make change purposeful and don't leave it to chance.

Change Leader

Let's start with the change leaders. These are the people who sponsor and validate the project that's causing the change to occur. The people who should play this role include anyone with target users in their organization. They need to convincingly portray to target users the reasons for the change and paint a vivid picture of what the end state looks like. They need to sponsor not only the goal but also the journey toward the goal.

To do that, change leaders need to outline for target users how the change will be accomplished, especially given their regular work and current culture. This requires the ability to speak passionately, think strategically and plan tactically. All along the way, these leaders need to remain visible, provide unwavering support and inject energy when momentum wanes. They can't just pop out on occasion to champion the cause. Staying close to target users is essential, as these leaders need to anticipate their needs and motivations, orchestrate people dynamics and earn the trust of the people they work with.

CHANGE AGENT

The second role that's essential to a successful change initiative is that of the change agent – the people responsible for planning, facilitating and implementing key change activities. The three activities most closely associated with this role are:

Connecting. Change agents have to connect well with clients, peers and change leaders. They need to be trusted, respected and likable, in order to influence via their own personal power. They also need to put aside personal agendas and exhibit respect for the people they work with.

Engaging. The people in this role need to facilitate conversation and exploration of the vision, while also making changes practical.

Guiding. Change agents need to foster synergy among target users, guide the plans and activities associated with change, identify issues among the group and help change leaders adjust direction when these issues become acute.

For instance, when leadership teams send out inconsistent messages about a change, it is incumbent on the change agent to point that out and help them frame a standard message. When change leaders aren't accessible enough – it is the change agent who needs to raise awareness of this and make suggestions about how to be more visible, like stopping by work areas or conducting listening sessions.

CHANGE ADVOCATE

The third important role is that of change advocate (also called opinion leaders). The people in this role can make or break the change effort because they have such strong influence over other people, both positive and negative.

To identify change advocates, IT needs to map out the political landscape and understand the influence dynamics at play – who is impacted by the change, who has indirect and direct power, who supports the change, who doesn't. We've covered all the skills required to understand the political landscape in Chapter 8 on Sharpening Your Political Savvy.

It's important to identify opinion leaders who are positive about the change, because they can help move things along more smoothly. But it's just as important to engage the negative influencers, as they could otherwise sabotage the effort. To get change advocates on board, IT needs to forge an understanding of their values and issues, their personality type and communication style, as well as the "what's in it for me" factor, or WIIFM. We then need to provide the change advocates with the information they need in order to get other people on board and request their assistance in making changes more visible.

SECTION 3
Clarity Precedes Activity

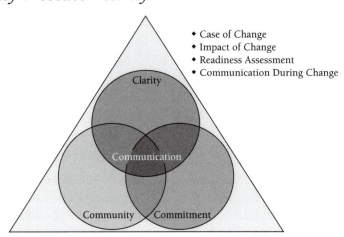

The third component of change is clarity, and there are two important elements involved in achieving clarity: making the case for change and ensuring the path forward is clear.

MAKING THE CASE FOR CHANGE

It takes more than a "good idea" to inspire people to commit to change. To illustrate this point, we use the analogy of a burning platform – many people won't jump into the unknown until they're really feeling the heat. Establishing that burning platform means understanding and being able to convey the business imperative for the change. In other words, why is the change necessary, and why does it make good business sense?

We define "business imperative" as being a situation where the cost of the status quo is greater than the cost of change. In order to get target users to make the leap to committing to change; the pain of the current situation has to be greater than the pain of making the change. This means that IT needs to be able to convey that the current state is no longer viable and why this is so – whether it's a new competitor entering the market, shifting economic conditions, changes in customer preferences or something else. Typical business imperatives fall into one of several categories, including strategic, financial, customer, operational, employee or regulatory.

Once you've clearly defined the business imperative, an accurate portrayal of the future needs to be painted – what does it look like, and what are the steps involved in getting there? What are the risks involved, and how will those risks be managed? How will target users be supported along the way?

Target users need to personally and emotionally connect with the change, which means IT needs to be able to clearly articulate why the change will ultimately benefit them – again, addressing the WIIFM. This involves putting yourself in their position, understanding their resistance and talking to them – in terms they'll understand – about what they stand to lose or gain with the impending change. They need to make a personal connection to what they have at stake, both positive and negative.

To drive this point home, we use a cliff analogy. Picture someone standing on a mountain peak, looking at another beautiful peak in the distance. How do you get the person to move from one peak to the other? As we've already described, the person first needs the motivation to want to move – the business imperative. But even when the person is committed, there's still a huge chasm he's got to get across, and he'll need support, guidance and lots of other help getting over the rocky and treacherous path.

If you can clearly articulate the business imperative and put it into terms that speak to the target user, you can more quickly achieve commitment. People who have a "why" will do almost any "how."

ENSURING THE PATH FORWARD IS CLEAR

Obstacles are inevitable in change initiatives. It is important to anticipate where those obstacles lie and how to eliminate them. That means assessing the impact the change is likely to have on various target groups, as well as the organization's readiness to absorb those impacts. During O&A's Leading Change workshop, people are exposed to charts and checklists they can use to make these two separate assessments. Following is an overview of these tools.

Assessing the impact of change involves defining who the various stakeholder groups are and then understanding how the change affects them, in terms of low, medium or high impact. You can do this by analyzing the scope of the change, the amount of change these groups will endure and how quickly the changes have to be implemented.

Some categories to consider in terms of impact include:

- **Knowledge and skill:** To what degree will they need to change their knowledge and capabilities to complete required job functions?

- **Processes:** Will they need to change the detailed steps of the work they perform?

- **Organizational structure:** How much will formal reporting structures within the organization change?

- **Relationships:** What changes will occur to the way groups and individuals relate to one another in day-to-day work, including teaming changes, political affiliations, etc.?

- **Culture:** What impact will the change have on basic values and beliefs?

- **Technology:** What changes will happen to the technology used in day-to-day work?

Once you've identified areas of medium and high impact, we recommend that you conduct a change readiness assessment. Change readiness is a measure of how well the environment is set up to succeed with change – whether the conditions for success exist. Readiness is dependent upon a number of factors, including:

- Has a clear business case been defined?

- Is cohesive leadership in place?

- Is there an attitude of willingness and respect for those leading the change?

- Are there sufficient resources for the change?

- Was the change designed in an open and collaborative way?

Looking at these readiness factors, you can determine which of them pose medium or high risk to the change initiative and then develop a risk mitigation strategy that will set up the change initiative for more likely success.

SECTION 4

Messaging the Change

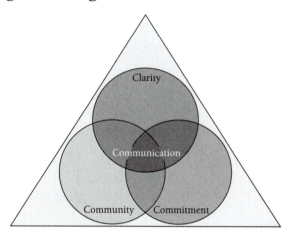

The last component of change is communication -- the glue that holds the entire change initiative together. It's how target users are supported through the emotional cycles of change. It's how commitment to the change initiative is inspired. It's how the change leadership community effectively plays their various roles. And it's how clarity is achieved to clear the obstacles preventing change.

And yet while leaders spend untold time discussing, debating, strategizing and planning, they spend little to no time effectively communicating those same strategies and plans. We often hear, "There's no time for communication." But, when you think about how much time is wasted with rumors, speculation and worry over what's going to happen or what's around the corner – if that time were translated into productivity loss, imagine what the figure would be!

Surprisingly, in our world of people interacting with people, communication is typically the weakest link. This may be because we all assume that communication is obvious. But it's absolutely not when it comes to communicating change. In times of change, everything that is said by the leaders of change sets an expectation about what the future may hold. People are waiting, wondering, reluctant, and potentially fearful, which can incite a number of emotions. These emotional states will impact your ability to drive productivity within your organization. That's why it's so essential to drive your communications intentionally and with purpose. And remember, communication is not an event; it's an accompaniment to life and to your change initiative.

Here's a good example of successful communication: When there's a significant systems outage, one of our clients applies more staff resources to communicating what's going on with the outage than they do to the technical fix of the problem. Their clients appreciate the communication so much that they actually think the problems are being solved faster than if all those people were working on the outage.

When creating your communication strategy, keep in mind that there are five different levels of communication. While many IT leaders use just two levels, the three less-used levels are the ones most effective at getting people to change. The levels most IT leaders use to communicate are one-way techniques, such as town halls, presentations, memos and videos to communicate in a unilateral direction with project stakeholders. Some might also employ two-way methods such as small-group meetings, breakout sessions and facilitated Q&As to encourage dialogue.

However, inspiring change requires a third level of communication, called "identifying implications." In this level, target users meet and have interactive group discussions about the implications of the change. Groups can be large or small, but the most important exploration is done with just the work team and the immediate supervisor. This interactive, multidirectional style encourages people to voice their concerns, which help reveal obstacles that must be overcome.

A fourth level is "gaining commitment," and it involves multiple small-group meetings which allow people to sort out their inner feelings and choices, as well as provide private introspective time. This type of communication encourages people to develop a personal connection with the change at hand. This isn't a one-time meeting; rather, it requires multiple returns to the discussion with peers, immediate supervisors or change leaders.

In the last level of communication – "altering behavior" – leaders demonstrate the new behavior that they expect from target users. They may need to use training, coaching and feedback mechanisms over time to ensure that the new behaviors stick. They should also provide plenty of opportunities for practice and learning and may need to reinforce desired behavior with policy or systems changes.

If you've ever found yourself wondering why a particular person or group doesn't seem to be listening to you, take a look at what level of communication you're employing. Better yet, determine which stage of the emotional cycle of change the person is in and you'll get an even better picture of what's going on. If you adjust your communication style, you'll have a better chance of getting through.

And remember that communication doesn't always have to be dry and direct. If you've ever taken a writing course, or even read the sports pages, you know that metaphors and analogies go a long way toward helping people visualize what you're trying to get across. This is particularly true when you're trying to convey what the future will look like. Try using narrative to describe a day-in-the-life-of the future, or anecdotes to describe the kind of behavior you want to see. There are rich communication techniques to convey what you see the future sounding like, looking like and feeling like.

CONCLUSION

If there's one thing to remember from this chapter, it's that change doesn't "just happen." It needs to be driven with purpose and intent. And for a change initiative to succeed, IT leaders, as leaders of change, need to understand and manage the four components of change – commitment, community, clarity and communication. Don't even think of embarking on a change initiative without using the tools, skills and techniques discussed in this chapter.

Many very smart people ignore these facts, spending numerous hours talking about their IT projects while avoiding the topic of change like the plague. Project status meetings usually include discussions about scope, requirements, development, testing, infrastructure, processes, training, budget, resources and business cases. Though these topics are important, so are the topics of change impact, communication, readiness, behavioral obstacles, risks and mitigating strategies, and commitment!

Throughout this book, we've challenged you to adopt new mindsets, grow additional skills and apply new personal tool kits to help you and your organization succeed in this profession. And it's all about change. In order to ensure that both you and the organization you lead are prepared for the future, you need to establish a culture of change.

Top 10

Ways to Drive Change with Intent

10. Every IT project involves change.

9. People who have a "why" will do almost any "how."

8. Know the difference between commitment and compliance.

7. Speak passionately, think strategically and plan tactically.

6. Conduct impact and readiness assessments.

5. Only "I" can change "my" mindset and "my" behaviors.

4. Use five levels of communication.

3. Know the emotional cycles of change.

2. Communication is not an event.

1. Change is personal.

SPECIFIC ACTIONS I WILL TAKE

✔

✔

✔

A Call to Action: Create Your Roadmap for IT Transformation

At the beginning of this book, we recommended that you identify the two or three chapters that address the areas most pressing in your organization today. At the end of each chapter, we prompted you to capture the nuggets, action items, etc. that you found most timely and valuable.

Once you've completed the book, go back through the chapters and select the items you are going to act on. Demonstrate your commitment to your leadership team and staff by initiating activities and showing your willingness to see them through. Engage others in helping you develop strategies and action plans to address these priority items using the take aways from that chapter. Don't forget to leverage the chapter you just read on Change, and your transformation journey will be well on its way.

Thank you for investing your time in reading *Leading IT Transformation: The Roadmap for Success* and our compliments to you for taking action to help elevate your organization, your team and your career to the next level.

Good luck to you, and please don't hesitate to contact us if you have any questions along the way.

Bibliography

Ackerman Anderson, Linda & Anderson, Dean. *Beyond Change Management.* Jossey-Bass, 2001.

Ackerman Anderson, Linda & Anderson, Dean. *The Change Leader's Roadmap.* Jossey-Bass, 2001.

Acuff, Frank. *How to Negotiate Anything with Anyone Anywhere Around the World.* AMACOM, 1997.

Albrecht, Karl and Bradford, Lawrence. *The Service Advantage.* McGraw-Hill Professional Publishing, 1989.

Albrecht, Karl and Yemke, Ron. *Service America!.* Grand Central Publishing, 1990.

Albrecht, Karl. *At America's Service.* Grand Central Publishing, 1995.

Axelrod, Richard. *Terms of Engagement: Changing the Way We Change Organizations.* Berrett-Koehler, 2000.

Beck, Kent. *Extreme Programming Explained.* Addison-Wesley, 2000.

Berry, Leonard L. *Marketing Services.* Free Press, 2004.

Block, Peter. *Flawless Consulting.* Pfeiffer, 1997.

Block, Thomas R., and J. Davidson Frame. *The Project Office.* Crisp Publications, 1998.

Bridges, William. *Managing Transitions: Making the Most of Change.* Perseus Books, 1991.

Brinkman, Rick & Kirschner, Rick. *Dealing With People You Can't Stand.* McGraw-Hill, 2002

Broadbent, Marie & Kitzis, Ellen S. *The New CIO Leader.* Harvard Business School Press, 2005.

Brooks, Dr. Michael. *The Power of Business Rapport.* Harper Collins Publishers, 1991.

Brooks, Fred. *The Mythical Man-Month.* 2nd Edition, Addison-Wesley, 1995.

Brown, Norm. "High-Leverage Best Practices," *Cutter IT Journal.* Cutter Corp., 1999.

Buckingham, Marcus. *Go Put Your Strengths to Work: 6 Powerful Steps to Achieve Outstanding Performance*. Free Press, 2007

Buckingham, Marcus. *First, Break All the Rules: What the World's Greatest Managers Do Differently*. Simon & Schuster, 1999

Buckingham, Marcus. Now, *Discover Your Strengths*. Free Press, 2001

Cantor, Murray R. *Object-Oriented Project Management with UML*. John Wiley & Sons, 1998.

Carlzon,Yan. *Moments of Truth*. Harpers Collins Publishers, 1987.

Clarke, Boyd and Crossland, Ron. *The Leader's Voice*. The Tom Peters Press & SelectBooks, Inc., 2002.

Cockburn, Alistair. *Surviving Object-Oriented Projects, A Manager's Guide*. Addison-Wesley, 1998.

Collins, Jim. *Good to Great: Why Some Companies Make the Leap . . and Others Don't*. Harper Business, 2001.

Conger, Jay A. "The Necessary Art of Persuasion," *Harvard Business Review*, May-June 1998.

Conner, Daryl R. *Managing at the Speed of Change*. Random House, 1993.

Covey, Steven R. *The 7 Habits of Highly Effective People*. Free Press, 2004.

DeLuca, Joel R. *Political Savvy; Systematic Approaches To Leadership Behind the Scenes*. The Evergreen Business Group, 1999.

Demarco, Tom & Lister, Timothy. *Peopleware - Productive Projects and Teams*. Dorset House, 1999.

DeMarco, Tom. *Controlling Software Projects*. Yourdon Press, 1982.

DeMarco, Tom. *The Deadline*. Dorset House Publishing, 1997.

Denning, Stephen. *The Leader's Guide to Storytelling: Mastering the Art and Discipline of Business Narrative*. Jossey-Bass, 2005.

Dobson, Michael & Deborah. *Enlightened Office Politics*. AMACOM, 2001.

Duck, Jeanie Daniel. *The Change Monster*. Crown Business, 2001.

Eccles, Robert & Nohria, Nitin. *Beyond the Hype: Rediscovering The Essence of Management*. The Harvard Business School Press, 1992.

Emerick, Donald, & K. Round. *Exploring Web Marketing and Project Management.* Prentice Hall, 1999.

Fairhurst, Gail T. and Sarr, Robert A. *The Art of Framing: Managing the Language of Leadership.* Jossey-Bass, 1996.

Farson, Richard. *Management of the Absurd.* Simon & Schuster, 1997.

Ferrazzi, Keith & Raz, Tahl. *Never Eat Alone: And Other Secrets to Success, One Relationship at a Time.* Doubleday Business, 2005.

Fisher, Roger & Sharp, Allen. *Getting It Done.* HarperCollins, 1998.

Fisher, Roger & Ury, William. *Getting To Yes: Negotiating Agreements Without Giving In.* Houghton Mifflin Company, 1992.

Frame, J. Davidson. *Project Management Competence.* Jossey-Bass Publishers, 1999.

Friedman, Thomas L. *The World is Flat: A Brief History of the Twenty-First Century.* Farrar, Straus and Giroux, 2005.

Gardiner, Gareth. *Tough-Minded Management.* Ballantine Books, 1990.

Gardner, Howard. *Changing Minds: The Art & Science of Changing Our Own and Other People's Minds.* Harvard Business School Press, 2004.

Gladwell, Malcolm. *The Tipping Point: How Little Things Can Make a Big Difference.* Little, Brown and Company, 2000.

Goldratt, Dr. Eliyahu M. *Critical Chain.* North River Press, 1997.

Goldratt, Dr. Eliyahu M. *The Goal, 2nd Edition.* North River Press, 1992.

Goleman, Daniel. *Working with Emotional Intelligence.* Bantam Books, 2000.

Grady, Robert. *Practical Software Metrics for PM & Process Improvement.* Prentice Hall, 1992.

Graham, Robert, & R. Englund. *Creating an Environment for Successful Projects.* Jossey-Bass, 1997.

Greene, Robert. *The 48 Laws of Power.* Penguin, 2000.

Greiner, Larry and Schein, Virginia. *Power and Organizational Development: Mobilizing Power to Implement Change.* Addison-Wesley, 1988.

Harvard Business Essentials. *Power, Influence, and Persuasion.* Harvard Business School Press, 2005.

Haynes, Marion E. *Effective Meeting Skills.* Crisp Learning, 1997.

Holden, Mark. *Positive Politics.* B usiness & Professional Publishing, 1998.

Jacobs, Paula, "Negotiating for Success". *Infoworld*, December 7, 1998.

Jacobson, I., G. Booch, J. Rumbaugh. *Unified Software Development Process.* Addison-Wesley, 1999.

Johnson, MD, Spencer. *Who Moved My Cheese.* Vermilion, 2002.

Jones, Capers. *Patterns of Software Systems Failure and Success.* Thomson Computer Press, 1995.

Jones, Capers. *Software Assessments, Benchmarks, and Best Practices.* Addison-Wesley, 2000.

Katzenbach, Jon R. and Douglas K. Smith. *The Wisdom of Teams.* Harper Business, 1994.

Kerzner, Harold, Ph.D. *Project Management: A Systems Approach.* John Wiley & Sons, 1998.

Knight, Christopher. *Top 7 Ways To Get The Most From Negotiating Via Email.* Top7Business.com, 2003.

Kotter, John P. *Leading Change.* Harvard Business School Press, 1996.

Kubler-Ross, Elizabeth. *On Death and Dying.* Macmillan, 1969.

Lancaster, Hal, "You Have to Negotiate For Everything in Life, So Get Good at It". *The Wall Street Journal*, January 27, 1998.

Lencioni, Patrick. *The Five Dysfunctions of a Team.* Jossey-Bass,2002.

Lencioni, Patrick. *Silos, Politics and Turf Wars.* Jossey-Bass, 2006.

Lencioni, Patrick. *Death by Meeting.* Jossey-Bass, 2004.

Lewis, James P. *Mastering Project Management.* McGraw-Hill, 1998.

Lill, David & Peterson, Robin. "Negotiation Tactics". *Personal Selling Power*, January/February, 1993.

Lundin, Ph.D., Stephen C. *Fish! A Remarkable Way to Boost Morale and Improve Results.* Hyperion, 2000.

Lundin, Stephen, Christensen, John, and Paul, Harry. *Fish! Sticks.* Hyperion, 2003.

Maitra, Amit K. *Internet Solutions for Project Managers*. John Wiley & Sons, 2000.

McCarthy, Jim. *Dynamics of Software Development*. Microsoft Press, 1995.

McConnell, Steve. *Rapid Development*. Microsoft Press, 1996.

McIntyre, Marie G. *Secrets to Winning at Office Politics : How to Achieve Your Goals and Increase Your Influence at Work*. St. Martin's Griffin, 2005.

Merlyn, Vaughan, and John Parkinson. *Development Effectiveness*. John Wiley & Sons, 1994.

Mnookin, Robert. *Negotiation: The Advanced Course*. Across the Board, 2002.

Morrison, Terri, Conaway, Wayne & Borden, George. *Kiss, Bow, or Shake Hands*. Adams Media Corporation, 1994.

Nevis, Edwin C. et al. *Intentional Revolutions: A Seven-Point Strategy for Transforming Organizations*. Jossey-Bass, 1996.

Newbold, Robert C. *Project Management in the Fast Lane*. St. Lucie Press, 1998.

Nicholson, Nigel. "How Hardwired is Human Behavior?" *Harvard Business Review*, July-August 1998.

Oakley, Ed and Krug, Doug. *Enlightened Leadership*. Simon & Schuster, 1991.

Ouellette, L. Paul. *IT at Your Service*. Kendall-Hunt Publishing, 1993.

Parker, Glenn M. *Cross-Functional Teams*. Jossey-Bass Publishers, 1994.

Patterson, Kerry, Grenny, Joseph, McMillan, Ron & Switzler, Al. *Crucial Conversations: Tools for Talking When Stakes are High*. McGraw-Hill, 2002

Patterson, Kerry, Grenny, Joseph, Maxfield, David, McMillan, Ron & Switzler, Al. *Influencer: The Power to Change Anything*. McGraw-Hill, 2008.

Patching, Keith & Chatham, Robina. *Corporate Politics for IT Managers*. Butterworth-Heinemann, 2000.

Pinto, Dr. Jeffrey K. *Power & Politics in Project Management*. PMI, 1996.

Project Management Institute. *A Guide To The Project Management Body of Knowledge*. Project Management Institute, 2004.

Quinn, Robert E., *Deep Change*. Jossey-Bass, 1996.

Rackman, Neil. *The Behavior of Successful Negotiators*. Huthwaite Research Limited, 1980.

Reardon, Kathleen Kelley, Ph.D. *The Secret Handshake*. Doubleday, 2000.

Robbins, Harvey. *Why Teams Don't Work*. Peterson's/Pacesetter Books, 1995.

Royce, Walker. *Software Project Management, A Unified Framework*. Addison Wesley Inc., 1998.

Sample, Steven B. *The Contrarian's Guide to Leadership*. Jossey-Bass, 2002.

Scheier, Robert. "20 Ways to Avoid Getting Hyped into a Bad Deal", *Computerworld*, September 23, 1996.

Schneider, Polly. *"Finding the Right Chemistry."* *CIO* November 1, 1998.

Senge, Peter. *The Dance of Change*. Doubleday, 1999.

Shell, Richard G. *Bargaining For Advantage: Negotiation Strategies for Reasonable People*. Penguin Group, 2000.

Simmons, Annette. *The Story Factor: Secrets of Influencing from the Art of Storytelling*. Basic Books, 2001.

Steinberg, Robert. *Chess v. Poker: What Is Your Style of Negotiation?*. Mediate.com, June 2003.

Thomas, Kenneth & Kilmann, Ralph. *Thomas-Kilmann Conflict Mode Instrument*. Xicom, 1974.

Ury, William. *Getting Past No: Negotiating in Difficult Situations*. Bantam Books, 1993.

Von Oech, Roger. *A Whack on the Side of the Head*. Business Plus, 1998.

Weinberg, Gerald. *Quality Software Management, Volume 2*. Dorset House Publishing, 1993.

Whitaker, Ken. *Managing Software Maniacs*. John Wiley & Sons, Inc., 1994.

About the Authors

Dan Roberts – Chapter One: Building Your 21st Century Workforce and Culture

Dan Roberts joined Ouellette & Associates Consulting, Inc. (O&A) in 1986 and has been its president since 1995. He strategizes with IT and business executives and their leadership teams across North America on issues relating to transitioning their IT cultures from reactive, technology centric, order takers to consultative, client focused, providers of choice.

Gwen Walsh – Chapter Two: Transforming Your IT Team

Gwen Walsh is a senior consultant at O&A, with over 25 years of experience in leadership development and organization reinvention. She helps clients create and sustain execution-based cultures focused on delivering results and attaining performance targets, shaping and instilling leadership competencies and behaviors, increasing profitability and competitive advantage, optimizing human capital investments and driving down expenses. Prior to O&A, Gwen served as CIO and partner for Christian & Timbers, a large executive search firm, and director of IS at Medical Mutual.

Anita Leto – Chapter Three: Building a Client-Focused IT Culture

Anita Leto has been a senior facilitator and consultant for O&A for the past 16 years. She has extensive experience in internal client service, IT marketing, consulting, teambuilding and leadership. She facilitates sessions for senior IT managers in the areas of strategic and tactical planning, GAP analysis and culture change. Anita is known for her keen ability to understand a company's existing culture and provide specific action plans on how to evolve to their desired culture. Prior to O&A, Anita worked for Canon, Inc. and Unisys Corp., where she held a variety of managerial positions.

Laura Gorman – Chapter Four: Evolving into the Role of Consultant

Laura Gorman is a senior facilitator and consultant for O&A, with extensive experience in the areas of leading change, internal consulting, client service, meeting management, and leadership. Her strengths are in facilitating the development and implementation of change management strategies. Prior to joining O&A, Laura was a senior consultant with a large mid-west insurance/financial services company, where she was a consultant to the IT department.

Lisha Wentworth – Chapter Five: Negotiating: Getting What You Want without Damaging the Relationship

Lisha Wentworth has been a senior facilitator and consultant at O&A since the late 1980's. She is an experienced IT instructor, course developer and consultant in the areas of IT client service, internal consulting, negotiating/communicating and marketing. Lisha is known for her energy, humor and ability to connect with and engage an audience. Prior to joining O&A, she served as a project manager at a nationally known health insurance provider and at a large New England-based insurance company.

Greg Fouquet, PMP, CCP, CISA – Chapter Six: Managing Projects — the Science & the Art

Greg Fouquet is a senior O&A facilitator and consultant, who has spent the past 15 years helping organizations in numerous industries improve the productivity, satisfaction and overall success of their business and IT projects. Before O&A, Greg spent four years at Ernst & Young's National Office as a senior manager and project director in the company's Advanced Technology Group. He also has more than 15 years of IT management experience, as vice president and manager of a 160-person IT department, senior group project manager, senior systems analyst and lead EDP auditor.

Charlie Duczakowski – Chapter Seven: Changing Your Requirements-Gathering Mindset

Charlie Duczakowski is a senior O&A facilitator and consultant who specializes in business requirements gathering and management, modeling, metrics, project management and business process re-engineering. He brings a unique blend of knowledge in the fields of system analysis and functional metrics, with a wealth of practical, hands-on experience in both writing and managing requirements. Prior to joining O&A, Charlie was a consultant for Capers Jones' Software Productivity Research. He also served as a director, business analyst/project manager, director of systems development and director of relationship management and systems analysis at Fidelity Investments.

Bill Hagerup – Chapter Eight: Sharpening Your Political Savvy

Bill Hagerup, a senior facilitator and consultant for O&A, has been in IT for more than 30 years. He has held numerous leadership roles and worked in the trenches of systems development, client support, and computer operations. He's adept at leading both software development and organizational transformation projects and demonstrates natural talents as an instructor and facilitator. Prior to joining O&A, Bill worked for a consulting company where he led numerous IT culture change efforts, and at a large insurance company, as vice president of organizational effectiveness.

Carolynn Benson – Chapter Nine: Marketing IT's Value

Carolynn Benson is a senior facilitator and consultant with O&A, with extensive experience in the areas of internal consulting, client service, negotiating, presentation skills, corporate politics and marketing. One of her key strengths is helping clients build a more consultative, client-focused culture. Prior to joining O&A, Carolynn worked for 17 years in high tech in a number of management, consulting and sales/marketing capacities.

Index

A

acceptance, 161
accomodators, 77
accountability, 35, 99–100
accountability mechanisms, 24
action plans, 26–27
agendas for meetings, 18
"agile methodologies", 96
allies, 130
analogous estimates, 93
anger, 161
appeal to a higher authority
  bargaining tactic, 80
approach, 4–6
"ask" mode", 115
audience profiles, 60–61
avoiders, 77

B

bargaining, 71, 74, 77–81, 161
BATNA (best alternative to a
  negotiated agreement), 75–76
best practices/processes, 21, 24–25
bottom line, 75–76
bottom-up estimates, 93
business acumen, 59–60
business and technology plan
  alignment, 25
business case development, 26
"business imperative", 165
business needs assessment, 25

C

Carlzon, Jan, 41
change
  clarity and, 164–166
  commitment and, 158–161
  communication of, 171–173
  community and, 162–164

components of, 169
culture and, 168
driving with intent, 156–170
embracing, 19
emotional cycle of, 161, 163
impact of, 166
knowledge and, 166
making the case for, 164
organizational structure and, 168
preparing for, 19
processes and, 168
relationships and, 168
skills and, 168
technology and, 168
"transition structure", 162
change advocates, 157, 163–164
change agents, 152, 163
change leaders, 157, 162–163
change management, 26, 96–100
changing minds, 159
clarity, 158, 161, 164–166, 169
client-focused culture, building, 32–49
client relationship management, 25
client satisfaction, 99–101
clients, 44
  building a client-focused culture,
    32–49
  client satisfaction, 99–101
  definition of, 6
  developing client loyalty, 38
  engaging in the culture shift, 47
  project management and, 92
  requirements gathering and,
    110–115
  serving, 99–101
  strengthening relationships with,
    145–146
  understanding needs of, 35
clout, 128
coaching, 24

About O&A

Ouellette & Associates Consulting, Inc. has worked with more than 3,000 IT and Shared Service organizations since our founding in 1984. *Leading IT Transformation: The Roadmap for Success* has been years in the making and is based on this extensive real world experience. The following are a few of the resources and services that our clients leverage in support of their transformation, culture change and professional development initiatives:

IT Leadership Services
- Organization Assessment
- Leadership Assessment & Coaching
- Strategy Development & Execution
- Project Advisory Services

IT Leadership Development
- Leading Change Across IT & The Enterprise
- Marketing the IT Organization Internally
- Collaboration in Action
- Strategic Sourcing

IT Professional Development Series
- IT as a Service Organization
- Consulting Skills for the IT Professional
- Strengthening the IT/Client Relationship
- Internal Negotiating Skills for the IT Professional
- IT Meeting Management
- Presentation Skills for the IT Professional

IT Project Management & Business Analyst Development
- Project Management Certificate Program
- Business Analyst Certificate Program
- IT Project Management: The Human Side of the Equation
- Advanced Project Management
- The Politics of IT Project Management
- Business Requirements Management
- Software Testing

If you would like to learn more about these customized, IT-specific services and how you can leverage them as your roadmap for building your 21st century workforce and culture, please contact us at 800-878-4551 or info@ouellette-online.com.